RETAIL DEVELOPMENT PLANNING

RETAIL DEVELOPMENT PLANNING

A COMPREHENSIVE GUIDE TO SUCCESSFUL GROWTH

BERNARD KANE

FAIRCHILD PUBLICATIONS • NEW YORK

Designed by Karen Wiedman

Standard Book Number: 87005-411-2

Library of Congress Catalog Number: 82-83043

Printed in the United States of America

For
Lois, Brian, Evan and Barry:
Contributors all

Table of Contents

Preface

Why do some business firms spread across the landscape in ever increasing health, while others perish quickly or go through a single cycle of birth, growth, maturity, senescence and death? The question obviously is too broad to permit a single answer, but consider one significant aspect of the situation.

Mass marketing has intensified division of labor to the degree where, as companies grow, management functions also become increasingly specialized. Thus, as a company expands, it becomes less and less possible for a single person to control or even comprehend all the elements of growth. At the same time, it becomes more and more possible that future development will be haphazard.

Those companies which manage to prevent that latter possibility from progressing through probability to reality are usually the ones which recognize the need to remain in control of the growth process by comprehensive planning.

The purpose of this book is to provide a blueprint for comprehensive planning which can be used by those who are responsible for the physical aspects of retail business growth.

It should be of interest and value to the corporation president as well as to the various vice presidents who serve under him managing the company's real estate, construction, finance, research, planning and human resource functions. Bigness need not be a prerequisite to readership. The book should be equally useful to the entrepreneur with one store and many dreams, for whether he realizes it or not he will for a time, as those dreams begin to materialize, combine all of those functions in one hard working brain and body. There is something of value here too, I believe, for the lenders, developers and consultants who service the needs of expanding companies. Their capital, time and energy should not be lavished upon haphazard ventures either. To the extent that it examines the thought processes involved in planning business growth from inside a company, the book also should arrest some attention among related sectors of the academic community.

A great deal of the material is presented in hands-on fashion, with precise instructions about how to do things. Where that is impossible—and it becomes impossible in places because standards of measurement vary from company to company—the technique employed is to pose carefully considered questions to the reader.

Attention is given to the many shapes which opportunity assumes. Since World War II we in America have concentrated inordinately upon development related to population and economic growth. We can continue to do so now only in areas where migrations of people and jobs continue to simulate factors which, on a national scale, have fallen into a long period of relative stagnation. We must learn to see the potential for significant growth in our existing facilities. We must learn to redefine the most productive uses of that space in terms of the desires and needs of a greatly changed society. That is happening already: the supermarket industry is involved heavily with limited assortment, low price warehouse stores in response to backbreaking price inflation; the fast food chains have gone far beyond burgers and fries in response to radical shifts in family structure and behavior. Finally, we must learn to recognize opportunity in unusual places: the static but still viable area which no one else is serving in a first-class manner; the once dominant competitor which has begun to slide into mediocrity.

Mass marketing has made bedfellows of many different type businesses in the sphere of physical development. The text employs a supermarket theme for purposes of continuity and brevity, but I have worked with promotional drug stores too, and would not hesitate to substitute that term throughout with only minor changes. The department store and, increasingly, the chain promotional apparel store, utilize different merchandise and less sophisticated display equipment than the supermarket does, but both type companies face many of the same circumstances and questions when contemplating a growth plan.

The most conspicuous newcomer to the group is the chain restaurant, and it matters not whether the food is prepared at a fast or a moderate rate of speed. If you're running a little restaurant in Annapolis, growing excited about the lines of customers waiting to buy your crab cakes topped with that secret sauce, the techniques examined in this book should help you draft a road map to Sausalito.

Introduction

Change is difficult to accept: we tend to carve out a place in life and then cling doggedly to what we have attained and all the concepts and conditions which made it possible. And yet change is upon us day by day, reshaping our lives and our works with all the persistence and power of the ocean rubbing against a fragile shoreline. Such force cannot be avoided, but we can escape being worn down smooth if we can isolate and study the components of change, and apply what we have learned to our future actions.

Coping with change is one aspect of planning, a step in the transformation of what has been and is into what will be. Planning is an activity which can have immense practical value or become an end in itself; an exercise which can be surprisingly simple or excruciatingly complex. It is a process which some use to decide what clothes to wear and others employ to control the life of a nation. Having such a large range of application and result, effective planning obviously should be a progression from input to product, set within the framework of well-defined purposes.

The supermarket industry can be a difficult place to produce plans which provide not only an in-depth analysis of the past and the present but also a program for the future. After all, it is a dynamic business run by dynamic people. Who has time for contemplation when the competition has just converted to a warehouse operation or begun to redeem coupons at triple value? Nobody, it often seems; but at such times even a few minutes of contemplation can reveal whether such tactics are part of a carefully structured plan or merely the desperate flailings of a mortally ill company.

Why plan at all? The fastest fork takes the choicest morsels from the platter. One compelling reason is the expense of development. In 1982 a 30,000 square foot supermarket costs at least $200,000 for the raw land, $1,000,000 for the building and site improvements and $750,000 for the equipment which combine to compose it. Add a few fees, and the total rings up at $2,000,000! There is no shelter in lesser tasks, either. Store expansions routinely cost $1,000,000, and remodelings within the walls $500,000.

Another reason is the different world we continually awaken to. It is important to realize that most of today's top management executives cut their competitive molars in the 1950's and 1960's, when store development planning more often than not amounted to getting somewhere first, and mistakes got rectified quickly by population growth and the still unmet need for modern supermarkets. But those decades are over, and any whose attitudes and practices still are rooted in them somehow missed yet another decade, when changes of major scope hit the industry with a force which could dominate its developmental aspects for the balance of this century.

The 1970's were, generally, a decade of runaway inflation and social upheaval. Inflation bit us in every phase of development— land, labor, materials, equipment and financing. Sometimes we faced those elements directly, more often we saw them translated into rental figures which at first seemed preposterous. And after we raised the rafters, cut the ribbon and passed the first can of peas under the scanning wand, inflation snarled and fastened its jaws upon our legs again. We paid more and more and more for energy, labor and the costs of financing the continuity of our operations. While those things were happening, at least within touch and some degree of control, the society which we fed, and which in turn fed us, changed to a radical degree. The birth rate dropped precipitously; family formations plunged downward with it; women entered the work force in great numbers and with permanent intentions; the restaurant industry, particularly its fast food segment, threatened to make the family kitchen obsolete.

All those changes hit with especially stunning impact in the Northeast and Midwest, where stagnant and in some places declining population and economic bases introduced the supermarket industry to the problems of overstoring. The South and the West, still growing because of in-migration of people and industry, became El Dorado, golden frontiers where the spirit of the Fifties and Sixties could be unleashed again. But those who went there discovered quickly that inflation and social change knew no boundaries, and that growth had attracted swarms of large companies with deep financial and management resources.

The ability to survive and prosper in the Eighties, and beyond, is going to be measured to a significant degree by how well a company, large or small, plans its development. Within each company that imperative will weigh upon even the most impetuous of personalities, and it will apply whether operations are based in Tucson or Toledo. Those who thump chests and pound desks will descend to routine tasks; those who make sense rather than noise will rise to leadership.

A good place to begin is to realize that business planning has little to do with ideology: the most fervent capitalist can become a practitioner without shame or guilt. If that profundity can be absorbed, avoid serious love affairs with computers at moments of major decision. The Grand Machine is meant to be man's servant and should speak only when spoken to; a few carefully considered questions should suffice. When the data grows deep, remember to strive for simplicity and practicality. One way to do that is to meditate for a day at the mountains or seashore. Another is to organize the effort into two general phases characterized by the following questions:

- What are we?

  and

- What do we want to become?
- How do we get there?

Part One

What Are We, and What Do We Want To Become?

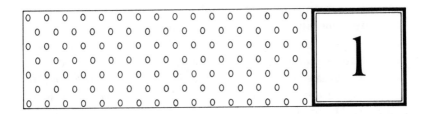

The Existing Physical Structure

What are we? The search for honest and complete answers to that question may be the most difficult part of the planning program. Too often a company has forged ahead and galloped toward a dimly perceived destiny. Too often, when and if it has paused to contemplate the direction and flow of things, it has looked at this question in the single dimension of imagery. Come to terms with the mirror image last: it is really the sum of all inputs—physical, financial and human—and a deception if viewed otherwise.

STORE FACILITIES

Physical evidence of what you are lies all over the landscape in the form of the supermarkets your company has in one way or another developed over the years. Take a long and critical look at them: if a person is to a significant degree what he eats, so too a company is measured by what it has built.

Unless yours is a small company—20 supermarkets or less—you'll need help assembling information and opinions about those stores. The greater the number of people who become involved the greater is the danger of a drift in objectivity, so keep the focus sharp. And be totally aware at this point that there is no substitute for actually seeing the stores and places involved; all of them if possible, a representative cross section if otherwise. If, for example, store #40 has become merely an operating statement in your hands, it's time to tear away from the perceptual paralysis of management-by-meeting and look at the physical quantity. If Rock Springs, Wyoming is part of your territory and you haven't been there for five years, you'd better saddle up the horse and see what's happened and is happening there.

A number of questions will demand answers, and it will be a good idea to record those answers in retrievable form.

Do the *sizes* of your stores reflect a conscious development of ideas over a period of time, or are they to a greater degree expressions of external forces such as the developer, the competition, the community or the particular plots of land involved? If the last six markets you've built have been 30,000 square-footers, is that because you need that size to express carefully developed operating formulas, or is it what has been handed to you? Do you feel that your stores of less than a specific size are not and will not be adequate? If you do, do you know precisely why?

Within those stores, whatever their sizes may be, is there any *uniformity* of layout, decor, lighting, fixtures, facade, signs and support equipment? In a large company there inevitably will be an assortment of concepts reflecting the passage of time and executive regimes, but do the newest half-dozen or so stores bear some resemblance to each other? If not, perhaps each store is being designed from the ground up, a process which is not only expensive but also indicative of a company groping for an identity or blindly following the competition. Are you happy with what you have? Have you resolved the sales/energy debates of multi-deck versus cabinet style frozen food cases, fluorescent strip versus metal arc lighting, conventional versus air curtain doors? Has the heat reclaim system truly recaptured its initial cost for you? Are you ready for scanning systems? Remember that the answers to such questions should relate to your own experience and goals, and not to the notion that a particular concept has become standard in the industry.

Do the *cities and towns* where you have supermarkets say anything about what you've been trying to do? Have you consciously gone into some while bypassing others, and if so, why? Is yours a company which has tackled urban and rural settings alike, or has it concentrated upon one and avoided the other? Is your presence in the communities you serve related to their economic and social structures and the way you feel about those factors? Is that total presence—your territory—related to geographical factors: highways and open spaces which lead onward, rivers and mountains and political boundaries which tend to draw lines?

Within those cities and towns, are the *location types* that you have an expression of what you've wanted and gone after, or merely a statement about what was available? Are you heavily concentrated in strip shopping centers, or have you tended to go it alone in neighborhoods and older business districts? In what types of locations have you experienced and are you experiencing the best performances? If a pattern of success or failure can be related to location type, the application of such experience to future plans is obvious.

At this point you should have a feel for the physical and geographical scope of your retail units, and can turn to something more familiar—*operating performance*. More than likely, the sales and earnings history of each store is for better or worse burned into your brain; but think of those aspects, if you haven't before, in specific physical and geographic terms. Are you performing better in certain size stores, types of locations and cities than you are in others? Do you perform well against certain competitors, but not against others? What you should look for, again, is patterns of performance which can be related to specific factors. If you can identify a few of those, you needn't ever throw a figurative dart at a map again.

Do you think of operating performance in terms of single stores, or do you think of it in groups which represent your company's true and total performance in a larger area with cohesive character-istics? That is, do you divide your territory into distinct geographi-cal trade areas and measure the share of market performance registered by the cluster of stores which you have in each one? If you don't, you should. Store #40 may be a smasher, but if it has three sister units dragging anchor in the same trade area the celebration should be postponed.

Finally, with respect to your stores, which do you *own* and which do you *lease*? The owned property obviously offers a great deal of flexibility, in that improvements can be made without soliciting the consent of the landlord and then paying him in some fashion for that consent. But even so, will the size and shape of that owned property permit whatever expansion might be desired, and are there any hostile building, zoning or environmental codes to be considered? If you haven't left the office yet, you can see that you will. The same questions have to be asked and answered about leased properties, but you also will need a summary of lease terms for each one. If such summaries do not exist, pry your real estate manager away from his deal-making to prepare them, and both of you will be surprised at what you learn. You will need to have precise information about:

1. Expiration date of present lease term.

2. Rent, % rent, tax, repair and maintenance obligations.

3. Number and length of renewal options.

4. Terms of the renewal options.

5. Alteration and expansion rights.

6. Use restrictions, if any.

COMPETITION

No appraisal of physical factors is complete without a thorough consideration of competition, because what you are has been both shaped and limited to a significant degree by the presence and nature of your business adversaries. Who are they; where are they; what are they? Probe those questions in all the dimensions of the study contemplated for your own company. It is interesting to discover that the other guy is not always 12 feet tall; that he too sometimes knots his own shoelaces together. You just might discover that you've stayed out of a particular city for the past 20 years because your Uncle Murray had an obsessive fear of Amalgamated's deli departments. On the other hand, you just might confirm the suspicion that you're up against a local juggernaut, and should continue to direct your energies and capital elsewhere. It is especially important to identify those competitors with staying power, those who with their talents and resources have dogged your efforts over the years. Relate your identity to them, because you'll have to contend with them in the years ahead. It is human nature to turn one's head toward the source of loudest noise, but that fellow banging upon an assortment of promotional pans, that meteorite in tonight's competitive sky, may be gone or transformed by tomorrow.

This, be aware, is for the most part a generalized analysis of the competition. Later on it will be important to inventory competitive facilities in detail.

SUPPORT FACILITIES

The physical inventory must encompass support facilities too, for they are a significant slice of what constitutes the present moment. Foremost, of course, is the *distribution base,* or in multi-divisional companies, bases. Returning to the singular for simplicity, is it yours or is it someone else's? If the distribution facility which services your supermarkets belongs to another company, it is time for a thorough appraisal of the relationship. In a company's physical youth it has no choice but to utilize the services of the best wholesaler it can find within or near its territory. But when the youngster has grown to be a 20-store operation and annual sales are counted in the hundreds of millions, thoughts turn inevitably toward its own distribution base.

Such a facility with your own company's name on it is a great psychological comfort: at last you control your destiny to the fullest degree possible. But before you decide to seize that destiny, look at that external supplier with extreme objectivity. Has it had the total physical capacity to service your needs over the years, and will it be able to accommodate the growth you're starting to plan? Has it been an efficient and progressive firm, or has its mentality been multi-story? Is it in a sense asking you how it can help build new roads, or is it basically preoccupied with its own objectives? If your conclusion is that the relationship cannot meet future requirements, there is yet another consideration. Before you make a commitment to your own distribution base, the multiple components of which will be treated later on, be sure that your problem can't be solved simply by finding a new supplier whose capacities match your need in all respects.

If, on the other hand, your distribution base is your own, begin contemplation by asking whether you own it or lease it. If you own it outright and your sense of security is strong, you may be sitting on a mountain of capital which can be made liquid through a sale-leaseback transaction. More about that later on; for the moment, ask yourself what you own. Has your distribution base—in all its dimensions of size, equipment and personnel—been a catalyst in your company's growth or a hindrance to it? Does it have the capacity to service a greatly expanded company, or is it near to its limit now? If building expansion seems to be necessary—and be fully certain that it is—do you have the additional land required, and if not can you acquire it?

If your distribution base is leased, schedule a quiet hour or two to read that lease from cover to cover. Don't leave that important task solely to your attorney. Most of a lease can be comprehended easily by anyone who holds a senior management position. How much longer does the term of that lease run, and what dollar obligations does it place upon you as tenant? Do you have options to renew the lease, and if so for how long and upon what terms? What rights do you have to expand the building facilities, if any? Who is your landlord, and what have your relations with him, her or it been like?

Very often a distribution base is not the only support facility to think about. If you have your own warehouse, you'll most likely have your own *truck fleet*. Is it up to date, well maintained equipment, or does it represent an enormous investment requirement about to fall upon your head? Do you own the fleet or do you lease it, and how pleasant or unpleasant has the experience been in either circumstance? If you're going to grow, your truck fleet will have to grow also, so you'd better come to grips once and for all with the dilemma of whether to own or to lease. Unless, of course, you choose to hand the whole situation to a contract hauler, which you'll do only after having stared at the bedroom ceiling for many a night.

Perhaps you have your own *bakery, dairy* or *meat operation,* or a *processing plant* which produces things like potato chips or canned nuts or preserves. And don't be surprised if you find a *data processing operation,* which began with a single terminal and is now a separate building crammed with expensive equipment and a staff to match.

Why do you have each of those facilities as they may appear? Has each been an integral but always subordinate component of your company's growth? Or have you been signing store leases all these years mainly to provide shelf space for the bread and cheese and ice cream and canned beans which your company manufactures? Is the data which is being processed only that which is vital to the conduct of your company's business, or has the production of data become an end in itself? If you're going to grow in a healthy fashion, you'll have to decide whether you'll want to keep and possibly expand such facilities, or whether you'll be better off hiring the services of outside specialists. Don't ever have too much pride to conclude that your bakery operation has been an awful drag upon the company. Someone else can do a fine job with your private label baking, and you may be able to convert a property asset into a million or more dollars of development capital. On the other hand, don't be a fool and liquidate something which always has been a unique component of your success with the consumer.

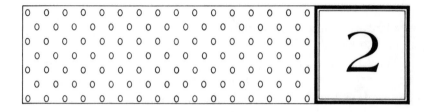

The Existing Financial Structure

Financial evidence of what you are is summarized most concisely on your balance sheet, earnings and operating statements, but now is a good time to think about the things you've done in development activity which have affected the current appearance of those documents.

PAST EXPENDITURE PATTERNS

How much capital did your company expend upon property, plant and equipment during each of the last five years? Was it a fairly constant sum each year, or was there an extraordinary expenditure in a given year? If there was a sizeable blip, do you remember what it represented and why the decision was made to spend so heavily?

What types of improvements did your capital buy? How many new stores; how many expanded stores; how many remodeled stores? Was there a fairly consistent numerical pattern year after year? What was the ratio of spending for stores versus spending for support facilities? Was that ratio consistent year after year?

What, exactly, was all the money spent upon? If you don't remember in fair detail, the chances are strong that it flew around like buckshot. Was your principal goal to build new stores or to remodel old ones? Some of both, you say? Perhaps you can explain why your company remodeled its store in Boomboro three times in eight years. Yes, it's a growth area, but your supermarket there has never had a completed appearance. Have you ever wondered if a single, comprehensive $500,000 remodeling every eight years might not be more productive than the three partial jobs you did? They cost a total of $600,000, you know. You'd rather discuss that later? All right, we will. You're pleased with the office addition at the distribution base; finally got the EDP department out of the cafeteria. Yes, you really spent that much for fork lifts. Amazing how quickly it adds up, isn't it?

How was the amount expended each year determined? Was it a two-step process of expressing needs and desires and then straining those expressions through the fine mesh of financial abilities and limitations? Did you invite your operations staff to submit its Christmas shopping list and then turn to your financial staff and ask it such questions as whether or not the cost of that list fell within the bounds of working capital generated by operations? Or did you more or less just pull a figure out of the hat, a figure which represented last year's expenditures plus a pad for inflation?

Where did the capital come from, and what effect did all the development activity have upon the company's short and long term debt structures? *Did* you develop within the bounds of working capital generated by operations, or did you finance working capital by the issuance of stock or the sale of debentures or a visit to the bank or the sale of assets? What you have done in this respect will have a profound effect upon what you can do. You may be in fine condition to start loading the artillery with heavy capital, or you may be in the proverbial positional dilemma: up to your lower lip.

THE MEASURE OF EXPENDITURES: RESULTS

What were the results of all that spending? Did your stores as a group reach the goals you set; are they now the market leader in your territory; did you move up from third to second place; do consumers finally have the image of your operation that you've been striving to express? If you're not sure about the answers to any or all of those questions, take heart: during the next five years expenditures will be goal-oriented to a degree which will make you feel like Chancellor of the Exchequer.

While it's important to know whether you're Number One or Number Five in the structure of your territory, you also have to look inward at the effect development expenditures have had upon operating performance and the condition of your balance sheet and other statements of financial position.

Sales growth during the past five years must be appraised several ways. The gross dollar and percentage increases don't begin to say much until real and inflationary growth are separated. Then there are the questions of whether sales growth was generated within an existing territory or amidst the fresh dollar bases of new areas; of whether gains represent an increase in the number of stores or the sales average per store. It is generally important to be developing sales in new areas, but those gains must represent a healthy growth of the overall structure. The company which during the past five years has added 20 new stores and $150,000,000 in annual sales may be dangerously overextended and in poor financial condition compared to a company which has concentrated upon improving performance in its existing stores and territory.

Whether that's true or not will begin to become apparent upon examination of pre-tax income performance during recent years. In this respect, raw increases or decreases are significant, because by the time income is calculated the effects of inflation have been confronted. Was pre-tax income performance satisfactory in relation to the amount of capital invested? If not, remember that it usually takes longer to generate income in new areas: your investment may have begun to mature only during the last year of the period. Beyond raw dollars, measure income each year as a percentage of sales. The whole industry does it, and it will provide a comparative measure of performance against competitors as well as against yourself. What is meaningful in this respect? The industry as a whole considers a 1.0% ratio to be important, but some large companies generate significant income below that level. And remember that the company which runs at 4.0% may enjoy factors unique to its own operation. It is best to concentrate upon your own goals and the historical direction of your own income/sales ratio.

We tend to think automatically of growth while appraising sales and income in the context of planning. It is possible, however, that by this point you're contemplating bracketed figures. If so, don't break out the lifejackets. Declines and losses, unless they are enormous and constant, may largely represent an absence of the planning process you're now striving to build into your company's future.

Moving to the balance sheet and related statements, the effects of capital expended for development are less immediately obvious than those of sales and earnings are, but there is seemingly no end to the ways in which those other figures can be held up to the light. What has happened over the years to total working capital—the difference between current assets and current liabilities? Measure it in dollars; measure it as an asset/liability ratio. That is one perspective, but what about working capital from operations in relation to capital expenditures for property, plant and equipment? If the latter figure has begun to run ahead of the former, future growth may have to be financed by borrowing or sale of assets, or both. If you've already had to go outside and borrow, to what extent and with what annual and long-term obligations? Another favorite calculation of corporate accountants is return on net assets (RONA), or the relationship between pre-tax income and net assets. It is a simple but comprehensive measure of asset management.

There are many other yardsticks—debt/equity ratio, for example— and each company seems to have its particular favorites. Two general messages are meant to be emphasized here. The first is to determine which measures of financial health are significant to your own operation, and to apply them honestly to your evaluation of where you've been. The second is to be optimistic about an occasional, healthy slug of debt. It is comforting at any given moment to contemplate statements which show strong cash and other asset positions in relation to debt, but that comfort never should be at the expense of the need to replace antiquated facilities or to grow into new opportunities.

LENDERS AND DEVELOPERS

In one way or another it is probable that your company has not been financially self-contained: your growth has been abetted to a significant degree by outside lenders and developers. It is time to examine your company's relationship with them.

The chances are excellent that you've done business for years with Monolithic Life or Sunshine Savings, and have refined the process of securing a loan down to a few pleasant luncheon meetings. May it continue ever thus, but chances are strong that it won't. Life changed dramatically and perhaps permanently for both borrowers and lenders as the Eighties commenced. Don't expect even the oldest and friendliest of your lenders to extend any more long-term, fixed rate loans in your direction. What you'll get, and only after a closer inspection of your plans than ever before, will be a loan which, if long-term, will be at an interest rate which either will float with and above prime or be fixed for a period but subject to review after that. If that prospect strains the relationship, consider that the lender also may look for a slice of the equities developed with the use of its capital.

Those same changes have been coming through in your relationships with developers, mainly in the form of rapidly increasing rentals and dollar-preserving devices such as percentage rental. Don't take out your frustrations upon the developer: by appointing him to carry out your wishes you've subrogated to him your position before the lender, and his only defense against outrageous lender demands is the stability of your company and the strength of his lease with it. Rather, concentrate at this point upon being very objective about the developers with whom you've done business during the past five years. Which of them brought to you the stores and locations you wanted, at the times you wanted them and at the lease terms which were most reasonable? As in any profession, there are the sharks and there are the human beings, and hopefully by now you've learned to distinguish one from the other. What you're looking to do is to select a developer or developers, in the context of your experience with them, and enter into a better-defined partnership whereby you'll entrust the execution of a portion of your plans to a person or persons who formerly operated solely in their own directions. It is as important a selection as you'll ever make. The alternative to making such a selection is the equally perilous step of becoming a developer yourself.

A final aspect of the financial status is to ruminate upon whether the company is publicly or privately owned. The direction of such thought lies mainly in future actions, but it is appropriate to ask now whether the company would have done it differently during the past five years if its ownership had been other than it is. If the company is owned publicly, attention should be devoted to the recent history of earnings and dividends paid to stockholders. A company strong in those categories not only commands respect in the investment and lending community, it also is in a good position to use stock as a vehicle in any acquisition which may have become a part of its plans.

The privately owned company looks at development differently: stock is held closely and is comparatively meaningless, and achievements or failures are relatively unknown beyond their visual presence. The private owner is generally envied for not having to lay his plans and performances before a coldly analytical public, but there are disadvantages as well. Borrowing usually is more difficult, and no man is more acutely aware of how many nephews and sons-in-law he has than the one who owns and runs his own business.

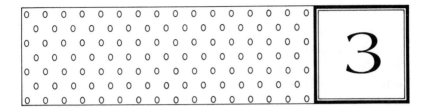

Existing Human Resources

The physical and financial dimensions of a company are comforting to explore, in the sense that one is involved largely with measurable quantities. That sense of precision diminishes, however, when analysis shifts to human aspects of a business. For that, be thankful. How *would* you put the calipers to old Fred in the next office? Is he a 6.2? Average plus 10? Rubbish and nonsense.

PEOPLE: MEASUREMENTS, MOTIVATIONS AND REWARDS

What needs to be done is to understand how human talents are recognized, developed, organized, applied, valued and rewarded in your company. Move into it from the birds-eye view. Which end of the spectrum is your company closest to: Personnel or Human Resources? If it's *Personnel*, you can go to a file and follow old Fred's progression from truck driver to Vice-President— Warehousing and Transportation, complete with a meticulous record of wage and salary advancements and dates of promotion. If *Human Resources* is the name, Fred probably is at a sensitivity session by the sea with his peers, exchanging insults or touching faces in a darkened room. Hopefully, you've got it all somewhere in between, an approach which blends a recognition of the human psyche's complexities with the methodologies of skill development. Do you know where your company stands in this respect? If you do, do you know how its employees regard the system?

One way to answer the latter question is to study the turnover rate at all levels, which is a very comprehensive statement about the total job environment. If the rate appears to be too high—and every company will score that differently—first ask whether it expresses employer or employee dissatisfaction. A high discharge rate can mean that your method of selecting people is shallow, or that your expectations are unreasonable. A large and continuing stream of voluntary departures, on the other hand, indicates that the company is neither a stimulating nor a rewarding place to be. If either condition of imbalance exists and goes on uncorrected, plans for physical development of the company may never get much beyond the documentary phase.

A low turnover rate usually represents a healthy situation: a profitable, growing company within which people are finding upward mobility and a general sense of fulfillment. The great danger of low turnover is mental calcification. Before you set sail toward new horizons, be sure that the old reliables on your staff have not lost the capacities which propelled them to their current positions.

There are many specifics which cause people to come and go. In this context they should be examined according to the job levels involved, separating those which are unionized from those which are not. What is important to managerial positions—both at the distribution base and in the stores? Money, for sure. How does your company's salary structure compare to the industry's? More importantly, to those of your most significant competitors? What about the whole range of benefits—health insurance, pension plan, etc.—again, against the industry and the competition? Who is in the profit-sharing program, at what levels and why? Ditto for stock options.

Sometimes it's not enough to compare favorably with the industry and the competition. Your company may operate in an area or areas where other type businesses siphon off a disproportionate share of the young, trainable talent just coming into, or just starting to progress through, the job market. If you're competing against glamour industries for people, recognize the fact now and do what you can to make your company attractive to those upon whom so much of your future growth will depend. That may require an upward revision of the salary and benefit structures; it may involve nothing more than a better presentation of what your company already has to offer.

Raw dollars are not the beginning and the end for most people, especially as salary increases lead to ever increasing tax bites. It is important for a person to believe and know that his performance and ability will be recognized, developed and channeled into ever more important positions. Does your company measure up well in this respect, or does it tend to hire someone and then show concern for his well-being and development only by the issuance of a paycheck every two weeks? Which description fits best is of great importance, for employee enthusiasm is a principal ingredient of growth.

MINORITIES AND WOMEN

Where does your company stand with respect to the hiring and development of minorities? Be honest, even if the answer causes the innermost spirit to cry out in shame. If the policy in practice amounts to tokenism by choice or quota by government mandate, your company's experience with minorities probably has been disappointing to the point of perpetuating fear and prejudice. The presence and aspirations of minorities will continue to grow in the years ahead, as will your company's need for ability and talent. Forget numbers and percentages: the task is to value contents rather than container.

Now is an appropriate time to grapple with attitudes toward what well may be a majority in any company—women. Too often, the majority is treated as a minority: note, for example, the use of the masculine gender throughout this book. We see the occasional woman store manager or buyer, but what horizons exist beyond those levels? Usually, none, unless Dad happens to own the company. Take the time to look around, and you may be startled to discover how many women with true potential for advancement still are chained to typewriters, copiers and other symbols of subservience. Yes, the rhetoric of feminism has at times become strident and tiresome, but one message demands contemplation by the company about to draft the blueprint for its future. During the Seventies large numbers of women made it clear that they were entering into business careers on a full-time, permanent basis. Just like men.

STORE MANAGERS, FRANCHISEES

Now that your hands are trembling, move on to the group which, if neglected, could be the Achilles tendon of a growth plan. The manager of a modern supermarket, especially the newer luxury models which cannot exist with less than $10,000,000 annual volume, must be an extraordinary person; someone who to a significant degree is running a small corporation which employs a hundred or more people. Face up to it, there are people on the executive level who don't possess that kind of ability. Where do your store managers come from? Do you have a development and training program which assures a steady supply of talent? Or, two weeks prior to the opening of a new supermarket, do you suddenly move the manager of store #28 to the new unit and thereby create a managerial vacuum at #28 or elsewhere? However you develop them, what do you then do to reward and advance your managers? Do you offer an incentive bonus tied to some measure of store productivity and provide the best of them with ladders to higher places, or do you treat them like draft horses? Plans and programs emanate from the office level, but the cash registers are, and will remain, out in the stores.

If your company also carries on, or specializes in, franchise and/ or wholesale operations, the need for evaluation of human qualities exists at another distinct level. In those circumstances, the company's fortunes are linked to an important degree with individuals who are self-employed, but whose establishment and growth will require the investment of company capital. It is easy for any individual to forget that his success partly depends upon your company's resources, so before the partnership is created, whether by contract or by the purchase of a new truck, his resources must be appraised to the fullest degree possible. More than potential for growth and advancement is involved: after an inventory period or two, that individual may owe your company $100,000.

UNIONS AND LABOR CONTRACTS

Unionized jobs exist mainly in the stores, the warehouse and the truck fleet, but increasingly at the office level. Perhaps your company is not unionized in any or all of those functions. If so, you probably enjoy a competitive advantage relative to wages, labor scheduling and the ability to communicate on a personal level with your employees. Take the time right now to find out what it is about your company, or the area in which you operate, that has kept you out, and can continue to keep you out, of the unions. That is especially important relative to growth plans, for you may be moving from an area where the unions are relatively weak to

23

one where they will smite you upon the brow instantaneously. Remember always that people embrace unions for the same reason they quit jobs: they feel that the company does not recognize and reward them adequately.

Where jobs are unionized already, the process of evaluating your human base becomes different because so much in the way of attitudes and rewards is set in the cement of labor contracts. Get into those contracts and find out not only what you have but also what you've been building toward. If a progression is evident you may be able to forecast the next round of requests, and thus go to the bargaining table better prepared emotionally. For three decades contract negotiation meant eventual capitulation to the most recent industry benchmarks. But in 1981 and 1982 a wave of bankruptcy situations, real and imminent, created a radical change of atmosphere. Now it is possible to do some serious negotiating upon issues formerly beyond discussion. The unions seem to be focusing upon job security more than upon wage and benefit increases, but management must realize that any advantages gained will become destructive if used in a heavy-handed way. Hopefully, the new business world of the Eighties will bring both sides closer to the realization that their long term welfares are bound together closely, and that to a significant degree they must become partners rather than adversaries.

Study those contracts also in all the details which may effect your growth plans. For example, expansion may involve the closing of some older stores: don't be surprised to discover that you may have some contractual obligations which will survive the closings. It is equally important, if the intended area of new growth is known already, to find out what you can about different labor contracts which may be encountered. Again, emotional preparation is important.

```
0 0 0 0 0 0 0 0 0 0 0 0 0 0 0 0 0
 0 0 0 0 0 0 0 0 0 0 0 0 0 0 0 0
0 0 0 0 0 0 0 0 0 0 0 0 0 0 0 0 0
 0 0 0 0 0 0 0 0 0 0 0 0 0 0 0 0     4
0 0 0 0 0 0 0 0 0 0 0 0 0 0 0 0 0
 0 0 0 0 0 0 0 0 0 0 0 0 0 0 0 0
0 0 0 0 0 0 0 0 0 0 0 0 0 0 0 0 0
```

The Existing Identity

If at this point you don't have a definite and rapidly developing sense of your company's identity, one probably does not exist. Despair need not attend such a conclusion. To be amorphous or polymorphous is to have formidable problems, but diagnosis is the necessary prelude to treatment and cure.

It is an extremely rare company, however, which does not stand for something to itself and to the buying public. A kind of spectrum exists. Perhaps you have just concluded that your company dwells at the wrong end of it; that your image—there, the dreadful term has been used—is one of small, old, poorly equipped and located stores with an inferior share of market position; one of eternal cash flow crises and steadily mounting debt, hobbled even further by a ragged distribution system and indifferent employees. If that's what it all adds up to, you are in definite and deep trouble. Your best and only alternative may be to apply a coating of bright lacquer to what you have and then fly off to Europe in search of a wealthy suitor. But then, you may have just grabbed hold of something with your fingertips and ended a long downward slide. Breathe deeply, and begin the long, hard pull in an upward direction.

If it must be one extreme or the other, hopefully your company is at the other end of the spectrum. Number One. The price and value leader. Model stores; radiant, well-trained employees. A distribution facility which other people come to to study. Lenders and developers calling for luncheon appointments. If that's what you are, you've already got your feet in the future, and please try to be humble in your dealings with lesser mortals.

Most of us live somewhere in the middle, and all the questions you've just faced and answered probably place your company there. The price image needs improvement, but people love your deli and bakery departments. Your stores are generally well located and large enough, but much of the equipment is antiquated. The warehouse is in great shape, but you count the trucks every night. Earnings are strong, but the company hasn't opened or rebuilt a store for two years. And so forth. Every negative is a plus in the sense that it has been identified. You know now in a comprehensive way what improvements must be made before the march into enemy territory begins.

Or perhaps you don't know, still. It is difficult at times to be analytical and objective about things and places and people and activities which have become the raw materials of your daily life. How to step outside it all? If all internal sources of information and opinion have been exhausted without providing a clear sense of identity and direction, it is time to call upon a consultant for assistance, to seek analysis and advice from someone who to an effective degree *does* stand outside it all.

The choice of a consultant should be made as carefully as the selection of a dentist. Ideally, the person or firm engaged will know something about your company and its territory. Otherwise, find a fast learner. This is no time to spend a year letting someone become acquainted with the operation. If you hire a firm, be sure that you will receive the personal and constant attention of one of its principals. It scarcely need be said that there is more involved and at stake here than what flows from a customer opinion survey. When the candidates have been narrowed down to two or three, consider personal qualities carefully. The last thing on earth you need is someone adept at telling people what they want to hear; a good consultant will, if necessary, slap his client's face with reality and fresh ideas. The importance of objectivity cuts both ways: once that outsider has been brought in, define the scope of his, her or their inquiry with utmost precision, and provide free access to the information required. The wrong consultant, given poor instructions and flimsy data, will function as the company astrologer. The moment demands a pathfinder.

5

Determining Future Directions

What do we want to become? Begin the second phase of planning with recognition of a very important fact: the company already is in the process of becoming something other than what it is today. That process never ends. What is different here is that the process has been stepped into and studied, and now will be given conscious, forceful and systematic direction.

Direction, in another sense of the word, is a good place to start. Should the company's development be basically an extension of what it is now, or has the examination of its structure created a mental atmosphere in which change has become an imperative? Move cautiously at this point. It is a very human tendency to desire a new suit of clothing which looks very good on someone else's frame. Before you decide to throw away what you have, examine it with loving objectivity. Nothing else may fit or look as well as what you have now.

Commence with decisions about the company as a total entity. Is this the moment to get into or out of wholesaling and/or franchising? Should you begin to draft plans for your own distribution base, or should you continue to use wholesalers as a source of supply? Does the rough outline of contemplated development fall within the existing territory, or does it lead into new geographical areas? Are you ready to diversify into such new ventures as drug store retailing or food processing? Can an accelerated development program be financed with internally generated funds, or are you on the threshhold of some fairly significant borrowing? If the latter, what is the best loan vehicle? When questions such as these have been approached and the answers refined down to commitments for action, the wheels have begun to turn in a serious way. They have not left the runway yet, but one's seatbelt definitely should be fastened.

The desire for change is likely to be strongest at the store level, partly because the stores are where new concepts undergo the test of customer acceptance, but also because trade media give continuing emphasis to the supermarket of tomorrow. Store size seems to occupy the most prominent position in articles of that kind, but the effective store planner will see size as a final consequence of departmental needs, and not the other way around. Said another way, don't start with a 40,000 square foot store and then try to fill it up. You may end up with departments you never intended to have, or stretched shelf space allotments which raise absolute hell with inventory planning.

The kind of store you want to have should be largely an expression of the desires, capabilities and experiences which have evolved and exist within your company. Trouble looms when the urge arises to copy a concept which is light years removed from your own. Is it really manifest destiny to build and operate combination or superstores, which add drug store and/or department store functions to the supermarket, in structures which range in size from 40,000 to 100,000 square feet? It may be, if that is the road taken by your company during the past few years. But don't do it just to wear the fashion of the moment. The larger the store, the higher the rent and other occupancy costs; similarly magnified are the potential rewards and risks.

30

The combination and superstore concepts seem to be most prevalent and successful in the South and West, where migrations are still simulating the phenomenon of rapid population growth. Another factor involved in those regions is the availability of land for development. Another is the rapid and sprawling nature of growth in many areas. Very often no community core exists or evolves, and it is in that type setting that the oversized supermarket—which at its largest and best combines many retail and service functions under one roof—seems to flourish. The concepts exist in the Northeast and Midwest, but on a less widespread scale. There the opportunities for such operations seem to be tied more to weak, antiquated competition and the chance to dominate an area. And in the older urban areas of those regions the size requirement becomes relative: an operation in New York City may be a superstore of sorts at a total size of 20,000 square feet.

If the decision is made to construct superstores or warehouse stores, or to move into any other concept which is radically different from that currently expressed by the company's retail stores; how will those older units be blended into the new look? Can they be? Will it be possible to expand those older stores, financially as well as in terms of their physical situations and locational values? No greater mistake can be made in development than to chase off after an apparition on some distant horizon while a dozen or a hundred stores in the 20,000-25,000 square foot range are crying for attention. A diversity of images is possible, but recognize the strains it will put upon all forms of merchandising and advertising activities, not to mention customer expectations. A diverse image really demands a diverse territory: suburban and growth areas where the larger, more experimental forms are commonplace; blended with metropolitan cities where older, smaller units are compatible with the total retailing landscape.

How will the new or modified concept be expressed in terms of equipment, decor, signs and storefronts? Equipment is being revolutionized by the realities of energy expense, and future equipment needs may be changed radically in turn by developments in food processing. If you think those old refrigerated cases will suffice for a few more years, study your recent electric bills. But before you make the usual plans for new equipment, sit down and have an objective chat with your frozen food and dairy people about sales trends and product movement in their departments. Decor and signs are stick-on features, but they demand conscious planning as part of a larger edifice under construction. Be aware at this point that decor and signs never should be the total expression of what a company wants to become. Storefronts. How many companies have spent half a million to renovate the interior of a unit, but not a nickel on the battered storefront? A fair show of hands, no doubt, from those of you who prefer to wear old tennis shoes with that $500 suit. Where that responsibility rests with the landlord, prepare to get on his tail. Convince him that occasionally his percentage rent should be spent upon something other than his favorite winter resort.

Perhaps the process of becoming a vision of the future will compel your company to become its own landlord. The expense of property development—land, materials, labor, professional services and the new world of financing which has evolved in the Eighties—has created rental structures which threaten to become unbearable for low margin, labor intensive operations such as supermarkets. Another factor bears upon this situation too. The company which has carefully constructed a long range growth plan cannot then sit back and wait for developers to fulfill its objectives at random. Developers have to start working for you as much as for themselves. If they can't or won't, and the plan calls for, say, six new stores in suburban neighborhoods of metropolitan Salt Lake City during 1984-1985, be prepared to do it yourself. And that's not easy. The company which never has wrangled with planning and zoning boards, architects, lawyers, environmental commissions and hordes of concerned neighborhood residents should double its supply of aspirin. The extra-strength kind.

If your company becomes a developer, your company also becomes a property owner. The American Dream. Depreciation and other tax advantages. But the investment required for land and building in a supermarket project now *starts* at a million dollars, a lot of capital to tie up in an industry which, relative to its earnings, has other heavy capital requirements year after year. Thus the vehicle of ownership must be well defined as to its purpose. Will it be meant to become a lucrative subsidiary, or merely the means of fulfilling a development plan? If the former, vow at the outset that the subsidiary will always remain subordinate to the goals of the parent company, and not vice-versa. If the latter, begin to cultivate contacts for a sizeable and continuing sale-leaseback program. Rainy day theorists will select a few outstanding properties and retain ownership of them for the long run. No argument there.

It is appropriate now to begin writing down words and phrases which give concise expressions to the major goals of all this effort. This type of thinking usually focuses upon the ideas of price and savings, but with a box of ordinary breakfast cereal headed toward two dollars, a more solid ring might emanate from terms which connote value, quality and dependability. The search, to be honest, is for a brief string of words which punches out the company's image in a way that captures and holds customer attention. Avoid P.R. excesses and above all be accurate. Nothing is more infuriating than to shop in a supermarket which fails to deliver what its catch-phrases promise.

The whole conceptual package by now should be nearly complete—items such as whether to own or to lease the truck fleet still must be attended to. But as the final steps are taken toward translating reflection into concept, impose two firm rules upon the shaping of what is yet to be.

The first is to concentrate upon becoming not the biggest but the best.

There is an unfortuante tendency in the industry to equate large size with power and quality; an absolute mania for charts and graphs which demand larger numbers year after year. Growth is healthy only when the whole structure is solid. The chain which plans to build 20 stores in an upcoming year mainly to exceed the 15 it built the previous year is sailing toward the rocks. The independent who proclaims his dream of owning six stores within two years would do well to focus merely upon opening the second one and the when, where and how of it.

The second rule is that once a solid plan of action has been worked out and embarked upon, never look back.

Equally important, don't spend a great deal of time looking from side to side. If your company's concept is successful, be assured that there will be competitors to the left and the right rattling an array of promotional and operational noisemakers. Whatever those may be—coupons, loss leaders, warehouse formats, you name it— don't blink.

Part Two

How Do We Get There?

6

Field Study

M any a fine planning effort gets abandoned at this point. Some people have the tendency to believe that the thing conceived is the thing done. Not so. From here onward hands-on work will become an increasingly large part of the program.

A reasonable place to start is to define every developmental desire the company has for the next five years. A Christmas list, if you will, a comprehensive expression which ultimately will be refined by good judgment and the limits of human and financial resources. Schedule an operations staff meeting—be sure to include district supervisors and real estate managers—and request the Christmas list by a specified date from each individual involved. In a small company the group which gathers will be very select, perhaps a committee of one.

DEFINING TRADE AREAS

Most people involved will produce their lists from memory and experience, but at least one person from the group should be assigned to examine every city and town in the territory which supports or can support a supermarket: generally, places of 5,000 people or more. That can be done by progressing methodically from one edge of the territory to the other, but before doing that it helps greatly to sit down with a regional highway map and divide the territory into trade areas. Each store unit has its own trade area: what is referred to here is a larger geographical area where several store trade areas exist within a boundary defined by unifying combinations of geographical, political, social and economic factors. For example, a company operating in metropolitan New York can work with a Westchester County trade area. The firm in North Carolina will see Wilmington and all the little villages within 30 miles of it as being distinct from the abutting Fayetteville trade area. In Wyoming, the Rock Springs trade area covers most of the southwestern quarter of the state, ending in some places simply where there are more antelope than people. Around Los Angeles the people go on forever, and a freeway is often the most valid trade area boundary when dividing up that area into meaningful sectors.

GATHERING MAPS

Upon arrival in an area, buy the best street maps available. In metropolitan and near-metropolitan areas that means maps which show the central city and its suburbs on one piece of paper and at one scale. Such maps are usually available at stationery stores, chambers of commerce, planning agencies and municipal or county offices. Buy at least two of each area, because one will become a heavily used work map. Zoning maps and ordinances are important also, and are available most often in municipal offices.

Most depict only one city or township, but they show in detail what types of land use are permitted throughout the community.

PLANNING THE TRIP

It should be obvious by now that construction of the work map in itself requires some planning. After purchasing maps, settle down with a telephone book and commercial directory, and mark upon the map the locations of all the business and government offices to be visited, plus all of the supermarkets. That in itself often constructs a route plan for driving around the area, but if it does not, complete the route plan before setting out. It is ideal to proceed with a team of two: one to drive, the other to observe and record information. If the task must be performed alone, drive and observe carefully and pull off the road frequently to record data. That information will be multi-faceted. One does not drive the whole route to examine population numbers and then repeat the trip to study competition.

Field inspection can seem, at the outset, like an overwhelming task; but remember that others need to know what is happening in an entire area. The building inspector in a community can provide a very good assessment of future housing development; so too can the planning departments of private utility companies. The real estate broker can be helpful also, but beware of exaggerations.

The information which should be plotted on each work map will include:

POPULATION

The population of every place in America gets counted every tenth year by the federal census operation. The 1980 effort produced a lot of questions about its accuracy, but nothing matches it in total scope. Some states conduct a census midway between the federal counts, and some counties and municipalities conduct a head count every year. Planning agencies don't go out and enumerate population, but often update census figures year by year. The point is, fairly reliable current population data is available. There are, in increasing number, private, computer-oriented companies which sell demographic data of all kinds, printed in columns or displayed upon maps. The trouble with them in projects of this scope is that they can become enormously time consuming and expensive unless tightly directed and controlled. Whatever the choice of source, get the population data needed and show its distribution, to the finest degree possible, upon the work map. In larger cities this can be done, if desired, on a block-by-block basis; in smaller communities the distribution unit usually will be the census tract.

Raw population numbers which represent a single moment in time are not enough for the continuum of long range planning. Trends must be identified, in their quantitative, qualitative and geographical dimensions. It is relatively easy to look backward and appraise trends leading up to the current moment. The 1980 federal census can be compared with the 1970 production, the most recent county planning study with its predecessor and so forth. The difficult task is to look ahead with a fair degree of clarity and accuracy. It is frightfully tempting to take hold of a recent trend and project it on into the future. For example, census tract #2520 experienced an 18.5% population increase during the past decade; it therefore is reasonable to project a similar gain for the next 10 years. It may be anything but reasonable to do so. The buildable land in tract #2520 may be exhausted; a developer might be about to switch, in the absence of zoning restrictions, from single family to high rise unit construction. If you want to know what's really happening and going to happen to population in tract #2520, a single rule applies:

There is no substitute in value for personal field inspection.

ECONOMIC CHARACTERISTICS

There are two dimensions involved. One is the primary aspects of the area's economic mainsprings. What activities provide the jobs; what kinds of activities are they; where are they located; what is happening to shape the future of those activities? The other is the way those economic conditions are reflected in the area's residential neighborhoods. Federal census tract data provides very specific information about income and housing quality, but doubts are increasing about the accuracy of what people are willing to tell the census. Again, the rule: there is no substitute in value for personal field inspection. The work map should be marked to show what type and quality of housing exists in a given neighborhood, and what is happening to those aspects of housing.

SOCIAL CHARACTERISTICS

This phase of the work can become a morass of data which never has the "so-what?" test applied to it. The federal census provides volumes of information about such items as age, family size, occupation and ethnic background. It is of practical importance to the supermarket operator. He will be careful to provide small portions of pre-wrapped meat and produce in areas which have concentrations of senior citizens and small family units. But there is no need to launch massive statistical studies of this type information just because it exists in massive quantities. The same operator will make some adjustments to his merchandise mix if he knows that significant numbers of Hispanics dwell in the trade area. He will do well to remember, however, that they also are, or are in the process of becoming, Americans; and that they have, or are acquiring, the consumer tastes which go with the term. The field observer simply should write down what he or she sees, and whether or not it corresponds with printed data available.

41

COMPETITION

A fair idea of a competitor's strength in an area can be had by glancing at the locational network its facilities represent on a map. As each unit is visited, various kinds of information should be recorded in addition to company name and street address. Of primary interest in this type study should be:

- Size in square feet

- Estimated age

- Estimated sales volume

- Type of location

- Type of shopping center, and co-tenants

- Expansion capability

- Special departments

- Parking capacity

- General appearance

A simple form should suffice for recording the data, with a space at the bottom for general comments and a place to mark the day's date and the observer's name. More information than the list above can be inventoried if desired. If it seems necessary to know the type and condition of store equipment and how many linear feet of grocery shelving exist—or whatever—write it down.

There is another dimension to competitive analysis which is especially germane to long-range planning: the possibility that a supermarket, a group of supermarkets or even an entire company might represent a desirable acquisition. The topic of acquisition is a subject unto itself, but for the moment be aware that in times of rapid, prolonged inflation, acquisition of existing facilities often represents the best expenditure of development dollars. The advantages of acquisition to the large chain seeking representation in new areas are obvious. But the process also works well for the single store operator or the small company, which may be delighted to find a supermarket which is no longer tenable by chain formulas, but is perfectly tailored to their own requirements and offers much more affordable occupancy costs than a new store. The general question to be asked is: how would this facility fit into the plan which we are now developing?

COMPANY FACILITIES

Your own stores merit as much attention as anything else during a field study, because many of them may be running in low gear, at one-half or even one-third of their full sales potential. Mark all of their locations upon the work map and record the same kinds of data collected for the inventory of competitive facilities. The effort is *not* superfluous: many top executives wear a groove into their swivel chairs and don't have the faintest idea whether or not store #19 can or should be expanded. Moreover, such people usually go wild over a good map: it seems to bring out the Patton in them.

POTENTIAL LOCATIONS

What constitutes a good location? People approach the question in numerous ways. An acquaintance went into commercial real estate after a nighttime flight: he observed that the greatest concentrations of bright lights occurred where major roadways intersected. Others require a system which resembles a marriage between Boolean algebra and computer technology.

In between lie the realms of common sense and the ability to comprehend an urban landscape. There are three inescapable factors—*population, accessibility* and *competition.* A significant number of people must be able to reach the location without encountering a great deal of traffic friction and/or an overabundance of good competition. That is the geographical approach: the good location as seen on the work map. Then there is the operational measure, which declares that a poorly run store will fail on the choicest piece of ground and, conversely, the well run unit will succeed anywhere. Many years ago another acquaintance, when asked why he thought his customers would shop at a proposed location with especially difficult accessibility, said "nineteen-cent chicken." The author of that remark obviously felt that it should be carved upon Mount Rushmore; his audience thought, then and now, that a bumper sticker would be more appropriate. The point is that most locations involve a 20-year commitment, and during 20 years many things of an unpredictable nature happen to the people who run food companies and the ideas which propel their careers. A piece of land with no serious locational handicaps will survive the transition from hot promotional pricing to a quieter mode of operation; bad ground will not.

The locational eye falls first upon a neighborhood, then upon specific properties. The practical eye rests upon the zoning map and code book. In general terms it is a waste of time to covet property which is zoned for residential or open-space uses. Attention should be directed to areas which permit commercial, industrial, wholesale or mixed uses, with the notion that any of the last three categories can be changed to commercial use without detriment to the surrounding area. But be prepared for surprises: recalled from experience is the industrial zone which permitted uses such as manufacture or recapping of tires. An attempt to rezone for commercial use became a special referendum issue and a four-to-one defeat. It is important also to understand the community: some places have zoning codes but don't take them seriously at all. Again, field inspection is the key. A jumbled mixture of land uses tells you that the community is run by entrepreneurial hip-shooters. Jump in if you like the hoot and holler approach to business development, but realize that your long-term interests will be served better if you produce something which will be a true asset to the community.

Remember when good locations came in the easy to assemble vacant 10-acre package? Like so many things in American life, what seemed to be an immutable facet of our existence has become largely a memory. Today's development planner encounters worth-while undeveloped land mainly when his efforts take him to the outer edges of rapidly growing metropolitan areas like Phoenix and Houston. Those are land bank situations. A visit to the phone company planning department may lead to the acquisition of a piece of prairie half a mile beyond the currently outermost row of housing. But more and more, tomorrow's desirable location already has a structure or structures standing upon it, and the task is to see and evaluate the ground which lies beneath.

Industry executives continually complain in print that good locations are becoming more and more scarce. They are correct where raw land is involved, but otherwise fail to understand how change continually transforms the urban landscape. An abandoned or moribund factory, warehouse, automobile dealership or railroad facility, if it is not part of a much greater decay, may provide a superb location for a supermarket facility. The same can be true of a school property. A decade of low birth rates has caused schools to be closed in urban areas all over the United States, and in many suburban areas throughout the Northeast and Midwest. Municipal fiscal anemia has since pushed many of those properties onto the auction block, and if zoning is not prohibitive in the near neighborhood, the notion that cash registers might ring where school bells once did no longer seems abhorrent.

Notes should be made about the physical characteristics of the locations marked for recommendation, including those which the rest of the office staff proposed. If aquatic plants are flourishing, spread-footers or pilings may be required to support construction. If ledge is peeping through the hillocks, begin to contemplate the cost of blasting. If traffic continually piles up at and around the property, lights and collector lanes may be required. If the location seems to have five-star quality but is still undeveloped, you'll soon discover the reason why it hasn't been. But whatever the difficulty, don't write off the location at this point: the object is to be comprehensive.

ROAD AND HIGHWAY CHANGES

The era of major highway construction is for the most part over, but maintenance and improvement work will continue at least until the Age of Petroleum ends. Thus it is important to visit the governmental highway agencies and find out what kinds of highway improvements are scheduled, and when. A single road change can create, destroy or significantly alter an existing or potential store trade area. The same can be said for construction or destruction of a bridge or interchange ramp, installation of a traffic light or creation of one-way traffic patterns. Highway engineers tend to be single minded about moving vehicles, but they usually are willing to share information, and just might keep you from building the Taj on the wrong side of the street.

When all of the foregoing items of information have been observed and recorded the work map is complete, and you have a document that is worth *more* than its weight in gold. Sheathe it in plastic, tape its edges, for it will be used heavily and often.

All the advice above about field study applies to existing territory, but it has equal application value in areas which seen to offer potential for an invasion by your company. Remember, though, that the study of a new area will take longer. You have none of your own stores to agonize over, but nothing else is familiar either, including the geographical coverage provided by various advertising media. Take whatever time is required to do the job right; be especially alert to factors which would make life difficult for poor but honest fellows building from zero share of market. Above all, remember that it's easier to contemplate invasions than to stage them. If you don't develop a plan which translates thought into action, your thrust into a new area will sputter and stall upon the beachhead.

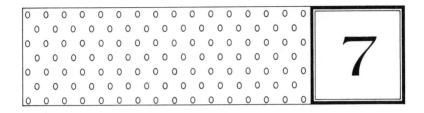

Prototype Store Plans

By now there is a feeling of forward movement, a sense of momentum. But several parts of the machine still need attention before cruising speed is attained. If several new stores are going to be built and numerous others already in operation are going to be altered and renovated to a major degree, what should the final product look like, in both a visual and a functional sense? Do you have something which passes reasonably for standard plans and specifications, or do you end up creating a new set of plans for each store? If your company is large there should be a corresponding degree of standardization. A basic principle of chain operation is to develop a successful prototype and then make a hundred copies of it.

To do so is not to embrace rigidity of thought and expression; it is to commence a process which brings complex and expensive elements under control while leaving room for incorporation of the changes which time always brings.

Some thought already has been expended upon proper store size and the type and alignment of departments within it; now it is time to give that thought the concrete expression of carefully drafted plans. Two principal elements are involved:

1. **Requirement Drawings,** which are also at times called "scope" or "guide" plans.

2. **Outline Specifications** for construction details, most commonly called "Specs."

REQUIREMENT DRAWINGS

Requirement Drawings should be prepared to a degree of finish fine and professional enough so that an architect can, within a few weeks, produce a full set of working plans for use by contractors. The major elements of Requirement Drawings are:

a) **Fixture Layout Plan.** This is the familiar birds-eye view of the store showing the location and size of all inside floor level elements of the store.

b) **Heating, Ventilating and Air Conditioning (HVAC) System Plan.**

c) **Electrical Plans.** These are broken into separate drawings which cover lighting, floor plan requirements, control schedules and a distribution diagram.

d) **Refrigerated Equipment Plan.**

e) **Slab and Sub-Surface Plan,** including trenching, plumbing and floor drain requirements.

f) **Cross-Section Detail Plan,** showing typical details for structural members, ceiling and roof.

g) **Finish Materials and Door Schedule Plan.**

h) **Interior Elevation Plan,** showing decor requirements. This is the most frequently modified element of the drawings, as it is cosmetic rather than structural in nature, and often is applied by the store operator rather than the developer.

i) **Exterior Elevation Plan,** including signs. This plan may be modified greatly by the developer and/or the governmental agencies which have jurisdiction over the construction process.

Production of a good set of Requirement Drawings involves a complex marriage of engineering, operational and merchandising skills, and in a company large enough to be designated a chain (11 or more units) should be coordinated by a separate department. Store Planning if the company is large enough, part of Construction and Engineering if it is not. The drawings are a lengthy topic unto themselves; only a few further comments will be delivered here.

FIXTURE LAYOUT PLAN

There is no ideal fixture layout plan. When the smoke of debate clears, some operators will always want their meat department along the rear wall, others along the side, and so forth. Don't get hung up in preferential art-form considerations; concentrate upon a good shopping pattern combined with efficiency of operations, a smooth and logical flow of goods from storage and preparation areas to points of sale. Also think about the future. If you need more sales area 10 years down the road, how and where can you make it available? Store expansions are dreadfully expensive under any conditions, but it's cheaper to move laterally through dry groceries and a non-bearing partition wall into a grocery storage area than it is to blast through the frozen food, dairy, meat or produce sales and preparation areas. The same is true for expansion into external space.

HVAC SYSTEM PLAN

HVAC systems were basically an add-on feature of no great concern while the price of crude oil remained at $3.00 per barrel. Now our energy intensive industry must reckon with every joule it consumes. Fortunately, equipment is available to match the challenge of the times. To cite one example, heat reclaim systems can recover enough spent energy from compressors and other mechanical equipment to eliminate the need for a conventional heating plant. But don't scrimp on the insulation requirements. And if you think that the problem can be avoided by setting up shop in the Sun Belt, go to Phoenix or Houston during the hotter half of the year and contemplate the cost of refrigeration and air conditioning. The point is that a small revolution has occurred in the design, function and capabilities of HVAC systems equipment, and as prototype plans are being assembled be sure that your engineering people know what is available and what is just beginning to appear on the horizon. Beware of technological overload, however. Don't be afraid to wonder if all that marvelous equipment might provide 150% of a store's needs; don't hesitate to demand that the system be in balance with the space it will serve.

ELECTRICAL PLANS

Electrical plans directly reflect energy concerns and have been ever since utility bills began to surpass rental expense in some stores. A great deal of attention has been focused upon lighting fixtures which are expensive relative to purchase and installation, but fairly inexpensive to operate. Equipment which offers a fast payback on initial cost through operational savings is always worth serious consideration, but be sure it does the job it needs to do. Food, whether in cans, boxes or bulk, is a colorful commodity which sells better when displayed in good light. Is it worth it to save a few dollars a month on lighting expense and have a store full of shadows and dark aisles? There are other cost versus payback considerations when drafting electrical plans. Where a utility company will permit it, your own transformers may save significant sums because of rate reduction. There is computer operated machinery which monitors the start-stop cycles of refrigerated equipment to insure that it runs only when and as long as it needs to run in order to provide a desired temperature. Other dimensions exist in the thought process. If your company is moving toward total scanning in the front-end operation, but isn't there yet, it may be cheaper to build those requirements into the plans now rather than to start tearing apart stores later on. Which will it be? Now is the time to decide.

REFRIGERATED EQUIPMENT PLAN

This plan wrestles with the major equipment expenditure required to set up shop at that dream location. Energy efficient refrigerated equipment began to appear about 1980, but prior to that it was a worthy companion to the American automobile. How fortunate for domestic manufacturers that Japan, Inc. did not step into the breach! Here, again, debates rage. Cabinet style frozen food equipment reduces energy consumption, but does it likewise reduce impulse sales by forcing the customer to reach through a door to get at merchandise? Not to mention the overtrained clerk who saves money by not replacing the burned out light inside the cabinet. Don't get lost in these debates. Make your choices and move on to the more important consideration of providing the right amount of equipment to do the job. During the Sixties and Seventies dairy and frozen food products and sales increased steadily, and so too did the equipment required to store and display it in the supermarket. Operating on the apparent belief that it's better to be over-equipped rather than otherwise, many companies created aisles where flash freezing affected peas, poultry and customers without discrimination. But as the Eighties commenced, those products appeared to be at their high water stage, with even a bit of ebb tide showing in frozen foods. Beyond that trend, the planner must consider that many perishable products which now require refrigeration will in time be packaged in pouches which will be stored and displayed on ordinary shelving without fear of deterioration. In 1982 it is still too early to draw plans around that probability, but it certainly is time to ask whether recent stores haven't been overloaded with refrigerated equipment.

SLAB, SUB-SURFACE, CROSS SECTION STRUCTURAL DETAIL, FINISH MATERIALS AND DOOR SCHEDULE PLANS

These plans are, more than any of the others, the domain of the construction and engineering people on the company's staff or in its hire. What should be concentrated upon here is to incorporate new techniques and materials which can cut down construction costs. And again, to be wary of doing and providing things merely because they always have been a part of past plans. The persons or circumstances which required them may have passed into memory.

INTERIOR ELEVATION PLAN

The Interior Elevation, or Decor, Plan usually excites interest and attention far beyond its real proportional importance. The right decor is highly subjective: one person's taste is another's amusement. The critical aspect of decor planning is to remember that it is basically a stick-on rather than a structural feature. The supermarket industry is a low margin business, and very few companies can stand the substantially higher construction cost of things like drop ceilings and cove lighting. If your company is not one of those which can, think of the supermarket as a box which can provide subliminal comfort and stimulation through the effective use of light and color. Light and color stuck on, not built in. Then when you get tired of your decor package after a few years—remember that both you and your customers will—you can merely peel it off and stick on another one. Compare that to removing a drop ceiling and discovering the HVAC ductwork which demonstrates that engineers as well as nature abhor a vacuum.

EXTERIOR ELEVATION PLAN

This plan, as mentioned earlier, will get taken over rather heavily by any developer and municipality involved in the birth of a new supermarket. That is no excuse to omit this particular drawing, however. Your design, well executed, may be good enough to provide the motif for the whole shopping center; whereas if you have none, another's taste will be thrust upon you. At this point the earlier statement about viewing the supermarket as a box will be retracted without an apology. Inside, the structure offers enough attractions to conceal plain lines; outside, an untreated box will look like one. The front, at least, needs to be softened and scaled down to near human dimensions by a facade which can be made of anodized metal or cedar shakes or anything else which can be shaped into a come-hither form. The sign to be mounted upon or into that facade will be your signature, so make it clean and crisp and of a style that promises to endure. Make it huge if you like, too; but someone probably will flash credentials and tell you that it has to be smaller. The topic calls forth an anecdote from the memory bank. Of a sign installed according to

55

city code and with a city permit. Of a virtual summons from the State Environmental Commission alleging grievous violations of its Grand Plan. Of a solemn trio sitting in judgment, announcing that "for the purposes of this hearing your sign does not exist." Of a decision to remove the sign or face criminal charges.

Finally, invest a few dollars in a landscape plan, which, of course, will vary from property to property.

Attention to the foregoing details completes the Requirement Drawings. If one size store suffices for your company, move on to the next task. If flexibility is required, go back to the drawing board and create larger or smaller size concepts, or both.

OUTLINE SPECIFICATIONS

The next task is the preparation of Outline Specifications, or Specs, which are the verbal companion to the graphic plans. Specs can be cast into an elaborate booklet or incorporated directly onto the plans, which gets the job done nicely and becomes a neat lease exhibit. Specs state *exactly* what kind of materials and workmanship will go into each phase of construction. Outline Specifications, like Requirement Drawings, are a topic unto themselves, and no attempt at full detail will be made here. Suffice it to say that they are vital. If you end up without ceramic tile on your meat prep room walls, or an inadequate layer of gravel under the asphalt in your parking lot, don't start screaming at the contractor or developer. You probably didn't specify those items in your requirements package.

UPDATING THE PLANS

Possession of prototype Plans and Specs, as stated earlier, does not impose rigidity upon the store development process. An important side product here, if such does not exist already, is a Store

Planning department. Periodically—say twice a year—the whole staff should meet and review what it has produced. If, a year later, frozen food needs have shrunk and there is a compelling need to create a flower department, the appropriate spatial changes and allocations can be made.

THE VALUE OF PROTOTYPE PLANS AND SPECS

Some will question whether the process, original and ongoing, is worth it. Here are a few reasons in support of it:

1. The company with complete plans and specs is ready to go when the best locations surface.

2. Working architectural plans can be ready by the time a lease is signed. The plans become a lease exhibit and the company knows exactly what its rental expense buys.

3. Rentals can be kept as low as possible by shortening the time between first exposure to the location and the start of construction. This factor is especially important during times of rapid inflation.

4. Leasehold improvement costs can be eliminated or held to very small amounts. Planning the store as it is being built can result in horrendous cost overruns and create the tendency to spend anything necessary just to get the job finished.

5. The thinking of all those persons responsible for store planning can be coordinated in a single project within a given span of time.

6. The process, once begun, can perpetuate coordination of thought and incorporation of new ideas through periodic formal reviews of the plans.

8

The Standard Lease

A necessary companion to Plans and Specs in the developmental process is a standardized form of lease. A finished lease is quite properly the province and product of a competent lawyer; do not be deceived that it can or should be done otherwise. But if a man would be a fool to try and write this contract which can bind for decades, he would be a cretin not to understand its structure and give it the shape of his own objectives.

Just as there is no universally acceptable fixture layout plan, so too there is no ideal form of supermarket lease. Nor will the standard form produced pass through negotiations unaltered. But do produce one, for the prospective tenant who can slap one down on the table at his first meeting with the prospective landlord may win a few terms in his favor right there and then.

The lease should be divided cleanly into topical sections commonly called Articles; commence with some descriptions of who is involved, what they are doing and where they are doing it.

THE PARTIES AND THE PROPERTY

The "who" are the *parties* to the lease, landlord and tenant, specified in very precise legal terms. The tenant will not be merely Cornucopia Food Markets, it will be Cornucopia Food Markets, Inc., a Florida corporation having business offices at 1221 Ecstasy Boulevard; Sunset, Florida. Understand fully the form your landlord assumes as a lease entity. You may have to live with that form—be it individual, trust, partnership or whatever— for 30 years. At times you may have to demand services from that form, even bring legal action against it. Will you be dealing with an entity possessed of substantial assets, or with a special creation possessed of nothing more than its equity in the development involved?

What the parties are doing is to create a lease between them upon a *specific property,* usually called the *demised premises.* The lease demises, or transfers, the power to use the property from landlord to tenant, set within a lengthy framework of rights and obligations. The subject of the lease must be described accurately, whether it is merely a piece of land, a piece of land with a supermarket alone upon it, or a piece of land with a supermarket upon it which in turn is part of a shopping center. If a building is involved, extreme care must be devoted to describing and defining the land area which is being transferred for use. If it is a freestanding supermarket, the entire land area should be demised. If the building is part of a shopping center, only that land which is under the building may be a part of the demised premises. If so, you must be sure to secure for yourself, your agents and your customers the right to use, in common with all other tenants, all of the remaining land area which comprises the total shopping center property. What is involved? Merely your rights to ingress, egress, parking space and service areas.

To be sure that there is no misunderstanding about the precise nature of the premises, a *site plan* which shows the supermarket, any other buildings, the common areas with total parking spaces enumerated and the boundaries of both the demised premises and the entire property, if they are different, should be prepared to accurate scale and attached to the lease as an exhibit. There should be no subsequent modifications of the site plan without the written consent of the tenant.

Where the parties are doing it requires a very precise *legal description of the property*, naming the street, town, county and state, then proceeding on to a metes-and-bounds description of land boundaries. This too should become an exhibit attachment to the lease. Getting bored by details? Talk to someone who commenced operation of a supermarket and then discovered that part of his building or parking area lay upon another party's land.

An assumption which underlies this descriptive entry to the lease is that the landlord actually does own or lease the property involved. Don't assume so; make him prove it. If ownership is represented, make the landlord certify that he holds clear and marketable *title* to the property, free of liens or any other encumbrances except as described—expect a mortgage—by another exhibit for attachment. If a *land lease* underlies his stated authority to develop, make that document itself an exhibit for attachment. These powers of estate must be certified by the time the final form of lease is executed, and if they prove to be false or otherwise fail subsequent to that date, the tenant should have the right to terminate the lease and seek whatever other remedies the law provides. The standard landlord response to a termination remedy is to say that his lender won't permit that. The tenant's response should be that there will be no lease without it.

CONSTRUCTION

The next major section should deal with the construction improvements which are going to be added upon the property. That should start with a simple description: a supermarket having exterior wall dimensions of 180 feet in depth and 200 feet in width, having a total area of 36,000 square feet. Then come the Requirement Drawings and Outline Specifications assembled with loving care earlier. Those, in the negotiation process, will be converted into a set of working architectural plans and specs which will represent the construction blueprint agreed upon by landlord and tenant. The final plans and specs should be signed, leaf by leaf, by both parties, and incorporated into the lease as another exhibit.

If the landlord has used the promise of a shopping center to get you this far, make him warrant delivery of that center. That can be done by reference to the site plan exhibit. If the store properties so described have not been constructed and leased by the time the tenant is ready to open for business, then the tenant should not be obliged to commence its lease or pay rent, even though its store may be by then in operation. This is a tough covenant for the landlord to swallow: what it usually does is to separate fantasy from reality while the lease is being molded into final form.

The landlord's construction obligations go a long, long way beyond provision of the building itself, and heaven help the tenant who doesn't specify those obligations in the lease. The landlord must provide, pay for, install and bring to the demised premises at points dictated by the building and site plans some very expensive features. Namely, all sewers, drainage and sanitary facilities; water pipes, gas mains, electrical lines and any other utilities necessary to the tenant in the conduct of its business. If a municipal sewer system does not service the property, the landlord must install and maintain a complete sanitary sewage system. If municipal water service is not available, then the landlord also must provide and maintain an adequate, uninterrupted supply of fresh water.

Shed no tears for the landlord: whatever all of that work costs will be factored into your rental expense as his tenant. Likewise for the cost of constructing the common areas of a shopping center, but nevertheless specify what is involved. We tend to equate common area with parking area, but it is much more. In addition to a properly paved and striped parking lot, the landlord must construct the necessary driveways, curbings, lighting facilities, entrances, exits, signs and landscaped areas which also are parts of the common area of a shopping center.

The landlord should then be required to secure any permits necessary to commence and complete construction of the demised premises, and to certify that none of the work is or will be in violation of any zoning, fire, health, safety or environmental ordinances.

All of the foregoing is sometimes called the *Landlord's Work*. A time frame must be imposed upon that work, specifying that it will commence and be fully completed by certain dates. The last date to start usually is 6 to 12 months after the lease is executed, and the final date to complete usually is 12 to 18 months after the start. Both dates can be delayed only by unavoidable circumstances such as strike, war, civil commotion, fire and unavailability of materials. Add Acts of God if you must; but what, exactly, does that mean other than an open invitation to create delays? In leases prepared by law firms where the meter is set at $100 per hour or more, unavoidable delays are often given the benefit of a separate Article called *Force Majeure*.

What if the landlord fails to start or complete construction of the supermarket within the dates specified? The tenant should have the right, though not the obligation, to terminate the lease or never to commence it. A further right should be considered also: the right to construct or complete construction of the supermarket, with the expense of doing so to be recaptured from future rental payments. If the location is worth the execution of a long-term lease, why give it up because a contractor or landlord defaults? These situations are very complex, and require the fine hand of a skilled lawyer to bring home the ship safely. The object here, as elsewhere in this construction of a form lease, is to explore some basic issues in layman's terms.

Construction normally involves some *Tenant's Work*, and, in general, the tenant's presence in and around the project. Therefore, the tenant should have the right at any time to enter the premises, in order to inspect the landlord's work and to install its own fixtures, equipment, decor, signs and inventory. Such entry should not interfere with the landlord's work, nor should it signify tenant's final acceptance of that work or commencement of the lease, topics to be dealt with shortly. Until the tenant certifies that the landlord's work is complete, the tenant should have the right to use water, electricity, heat, air conditioning or any other utilities in or around the premises without charge.

A form lease can't cover the many construction cost variables which can arise, but such material should become part of the executed lease. If for any reason final building plans can't be agreed upon in time to make them a part of the lease, uncertainties will exist about how the final dollars of construction expense will be borne. The landlord may agree that for a guaranteed annual rental of $180,000, he will expend $900,000 upon the construction of a 30,000 square foot supermarket building. If the certified final cost of the building should exceed $900,000, he will expect the tenant to pay for the excess either as a lump sum leasehold improvement or as an added rental at a predetermined formula. This is anything but a handshake situation.

TERM AND COMMENCEMENT

The length of the lease, or *term,* and the date upon which the lease becomes effective, or its *commencement,* are important statements.

Most supermarket leases since World War II have carried an initial term of 20 years, because that generally has been the length of time required to amortize the long-term, fixed-rate loans secured by developers. In 1982 we are headed into new conditions because of the new world which has emerged relative to permanent financing of retail developments. Whatever the length of the initial term may now be, just remember that every obligation which attaches to you as tenant must be fulfilled during the entire length of that term. You are entering into a contract which in today's society has become more lengthy and binding than most marriages.

The lease, obviously, should not commence until the landlord has fulfilled all his obligations to construct the supermarket and its related improvements. Thus the tenant needs the right to accept or not accept that work as having been completed satisfactorily according to plans and specifications. Very minor items, such as replacement of a few broken or imperfect floor tiles, should not impede the acceptance process. Landlord and tenant should inspect the work together, and summarize such minor items on what is normally called a *punch list*. The tenant then accepts the work as completed, contingent upon satisfactory completion of all punch list items within 30-45 days.

When the landlord's work has been accepted as completed, the clock then begins to tick toward commencement, and the tenant must agree that the lease will commence some 45 to 60 days thereafter—ask for 60—or when the supermarket opens for business, whichever date occurs earlier. The 45 to 60 day period specified is the time span during which the tenant must enter the premises and complete its work—i.e., the installation of fixtures, equipment, decor, signs and inventory. The landlord must deliver, prior to the commencement date, anything approximating a certificate of occupancy which may be required by local law.

The commencement date starts what is called the *lease year*. If it commences on August 10, the first lease year will be adjusted to end on the following August 31, and annually on each August 31 thereafter. It is possible for the first lease year to be shortened to end on December 31, and thereafter go on a calendar year basis. But then the length of the lease term should be adjusted to end on December 31 also.

Promptly after the commencement date, a short form lease, or *Memorandum of Lease*, should be executed and recorded in the appropriate governmental registry office. The Memorandum should specify parties, location, commencement and expiration dates and any other information deemed recordable by either party, but not rent and other charges payable by the tenant.

RENEWAL OF TERM

If the initial term of lease is a pleasant experience for both parties, they probably will desire to renew that relationship for an extended period of years. Thus the landlord grants to the tenant, at the inception of the lease, the *option to renew* it when the initial term expires. Prior to 1980, most leases granted the tenant the option to renew the lease for at least three successive five-year periods, usually upon the same terms and conditions which governed the initial term. If you as a tenant can still secure that kind of renewal option, fine; but the Eighties have brought changes to every facet of retail business, and this is no exception.

The landlord may request an increase in guaranteed rental payments during option periods. If he is to be granted, elsewhere in the lease, an excess or percentage rental based upon sales performance, tell him that excess rental tied to sales will suffice to protect his dollars against the ravages of inflation. If he wins the argument, give him a clearly stated increase in his guaranteed rent, but be sure to adjust upward accordingly the sales base at which percentage rental begins to operate. Under no circumstances should you agree to tie guaranteed rent to the Consumer Price Index or any other government statistic which resembles it. Such figures are total unknowns, lurking off in the future like potholes in a highway. To illustrate the concern, between 1967 and mid-1981, the Consumer Price Index rose from 100% to 267%!

Lease renewal should require a written notice of intention from tenant to landlord, to be served at least six months prior to expiration of the then current term. This in turn will require a company to prepare and maintain a schedule of renewal notification dates for all its stores. Some try to get around this task by making renewals automatic unless negative notice is served. But forget that negative notice and you get a five-year sentence in a store you want to close.

RENT, PERCENTAGE RENT

A very select group believes that rent is the only topic of consequence in a lease. Which kind of rent: *minimum, percentage* or *additional?* You'll probably meet all three in any lease.

A minimum, or guaranteed, annual rent is paid by the tenant to the landlord, divided into equal monthly installments, usually paid in advance. It is the amount required to amortize the landlord's long-term loan and provide him with a suitable return on his investment. In leases written prior to 1980 minimum rent was most often a constant amount throughout the original and renewal terms. In some old leases—O vanished Golden Age!—rent actually decreased during renewal terms because the parties assumed the mortgage would be discharged fully by then. But after 1980, inflation and the variable rate loan created a new situation. It is not uncommon now for minimum rent to change periodically within the initial term—every five years, for example.

The first payment of minimum rent should be tied to the events, explained earlier, which trigger the commencement date of the lease. If the landlord fails to complete the supermarket or the total shopping center by a specified date, no minimum rent should be paid until and if he does.

Percentage rent is an excess sum paid by tenant to landlord when its sales exceed a specified amount during a lease year. It is a major victory now when a tenant executes a lease which does not create a percentage rent condition, because the headlong tumble into double digit inflation after 1974 made landlords everywhere alert to the danger that the real value of a fixed rental could decline drastically.

There is no standard percentage to agree upon, even though landlords may insist that 1½% is the industry yardstick. Companies blithely agreed to 1½% in the Fifties and Sixties because it was hard to believe that the percentage rent sales base of a store—say $3,000,000—would ever be reached. Those companies now find themselves paying $75,000 percentage rent on a supermarket which grosses $8,000,000 per annum. Now that minimum rents of $150,000 are not uncommon, landlords may try to slide a stiff percentage rent past on the premise that sales may never go high enough to trigger operation of the percentage. Don't believe that for a minute! The $10,000,000 annual volume has become commonplace, and $15,000,000 is moving into view. Given the trend of utility and payroll costs, the tenant never should agree to pay more than a 1% excess rent. If nothing lower than that can be agreed upon initially, insist upon scaling down the percentage as sales volume rises. For example:1% over $10,000,000; 0.75% over $12,000,000; 0.50% over $15,000,000.

The language which defines percentage rent can burn the tenant if expressed imprecisely. It should be stated thusly: that during each lease year the tenant will pay the amount by which 1% of annual sales exceeds the minimum annual rent. If the minimum rent for the supermarket is $100,000 per annum, the 1% excess rental will begin to operate at and beyond annual sales of $10,000,000, since 1% of that figure equals the minimum annual rent of $100,000. The importance of expressing the phrase as shown above is that if the minimum rent changes during the lease term, as it is likely to do during inflationary times, so too will the sales base at which percentage rent begins to operate. Of course percentage rent may be defined in any terms agreed upon by the parties to the lease. The supermarket with the $100,000 minimum annual rent might carry a percentage rent obligation of 1% of annual sales in excess of $12,000,000. However the agreement might read, the tenant must remember to provide for upward changes in minimum rent.

Another vital part of the percentage rent Article is the term *"offset."* The tenant should win the right to offset certain of its occupancy expenses in any given lease year against any percentage rent payable for that year. Those expenses are real estate taxes, common area maintenance and building repairs. The landlord will chop away at the magnitude of any offset; the tenant should at the very least preserve the right to offset those expenses against half the percentage rent payable during any lease year.

The tenant will be required to report its sales and pay any percentage rent due within 30 to 60 days after the end of each lease year. The landlord may ask for reporting and payment on a quarterly or even a monthly basis, citing his income tax obligations. Resist. It's a bonus payment to him. Use the money yourself throughout the year, but be sure to have an accrual system in operation. Finally, the landlord will have the right to audit the tenant's sales records pertinent to the demised premises if skeptical of the sales report. A request for audit should be served by written notice, specifying a time no sooner than 10 days from the date of notice.

Care was taken above not to define percentage rent as additional rent, which is exactly what the landlord's lawyer will want to do. He will also want to define as additional rent any regular payments to be made by the tenant for real estate taxes, common area and building maintenance. Why he will want to do that will be examined in the section which treats defaults by the tenant.

REAL ESTATE TAXES

If the terms *"net"* and *"gross"* don't surface when rent is negotiated, they certainly will when the topic of real estate taxes comes to the surface. A gross rent is one from which the landlord must subtract his obligation to pay all property expenses such as real estate taxes, common area maintenance and building repairs. It is a condition found in a few leases written before 1965, but virtually archaic in those written after 1975. A net rent is one from which the landlord must subtract only the debt service obligations of his long term loan. It is what every landlord now requests. When a net lease ripens into payment of percentage rent, the landlord will serve notice that his mailing address has changed from Gelid, Michigan to Sunburst, Florida. Obviously, there can be many shadings of obligation between gross and net, but forget descriptions such as net, net and net, net, net. Rather, define with great precision who pays for what.

The landlord will expect the tenant to pay the full real estate tax bill and vice-versa. Write the vice-versa into your standard lease and accept any gift horses gratefully, but be prepared to pay the full tax bill as long as that expense can be offset against percentage rent payments. Sometimes the landlord will agree to pay, throughout the lease term, what is described as the *"base year"* taxes upon the demised premises. Be sure to describe that as the first full tax year during which the demised premises are assessed on the basis of fully completed construction of improvements to the property. Even so, expect that the landlord will attempt to load all or part of that base year tax payment into your minimum rent.

If taxes are not assessed specifically upon the supermarket premises, the tenant will be asked to pay its *pro-rata share of taxes* levied upon the entire shopping center. This generally means that if your store constitutes 20% of the total building space, you pay 20% of the tax bill. Be very careful to define your pro-rata obligation against gross leasable space completed or under construction in the shopping center, whether such space is leased or occupied or not. The landlord's inability to attract and/or keep other tenants must not become your tax liability.

The tenant should not be required to make any payment of its real estate tax obligations until it receives a monetary statement of those obligations from the landlord, along with a copy of the tax bill marked by the taxing authority as paid in full. The tenant should not be liable for any penalty or interest incurred by the landlord's failure to make timely payment, nor for any non-real estate taxes levied upon the demised premises, nor for any assessment against the same for the installation or extension of utility lines, prior to or at any time during the term of lease or renewals of it. When timely payment of taxes results in a discounted obligation, the tenant should have its share of the discount credited against its liability. Finally, the tenant should have the right to pursue for its benefit, with the landlord's cooperation, a reduction in valuation or an abatement of taxes upon the demised premises.

COMMON AREA MAINTENANCE

After a lease has been executed and a supermarket built and opened for business, nothing related to it will consume more of a property manager's time then ongoing common area maintenance.

If the market is freestanding and your company has its own

maintenance crew covering a compact territory, agree to do and pay for the work yourself: you'll save money. Under any other circumstances the landlord should have the obligation to perform that work. Since the tenant pays for it, be sure to specify what is involved. Boiler-plate items are the removal of dirt, debris, ice and snow from the parking lot; patching and re-striping the surface of the parking lot; maintenance of all external lighting facilities; care of signs and landscaping devoted to common use. Beyond those operational necessities lies a swamp which can swallow a tenant whole. The landlord may seek to include items such as management fees, liability insurance, security service, equipment purchases and subterranean utility work to the expenses attributable to common area maintenance. The list has become endless. Agree to include any or all, and the cost involved quickly reaches the lower lip. It really becomes unbearable when the supermarket is attached to a covered mall, and the tenant thereby becomes liable for a share of mall operational and maintenance expenses, particularly heating and air conditioning. When all unfavorable forces are in conjunction, common and mall area maintenance can cost the tenant, in 1982, up to $1.50 per square foot of store area annually.

Since World War II the burden of these expenses has shifted gradually from landlord to tenant. Some old leases still in force provide free or very inexpensive maintenance for the tenant, but in such situations the tenant eventually gets what it pays for—nothing or very little. Agree to pay your share of the cost of the work performed, all if freestanding, a pro-rata share if in a shopping center. The pro-rata share should be defined exactly as in the real estate tax Article, with emphasis upon leasable space. The landlord will press for payment based upon leased space, but hold firm on the principle that a fully leased and occupied center is his responsibility and risk.

Payment usually is made on a quarterly basis. Require the landlord to submit invoices which support the charges, or at the very least to itemize expenses by categories such as striping, sweeping, plowing, etc. This can result in a deluge of paper upon the property manager's desk, but the labor is worth it if the landlord by accident or design treats common area maintenance as a profit center. A recent experience saw a landlord take back $3,000 in common area billing for one year, one store. In an industry which labors mightily to earn 1% on its sales, that was the equivalent of adding $300,000 in annual sales to the store.

REPAIRS, ALTERATIONS AND ADDITIONS

These topics divide nicely into a discussion of rights and obligations incumbent upon the landlord and the tenant.

The landlord, as owner of the property, should be required to maintain and repair the structural and exterior portions of the demised premises. That obligation should be specified with respect to structural members, foundations and floor slabs, walls, roofs and roof coverings, canopies, facades and attached light fixtures, gutters, downspouts and all heating, ventilating, air conditioning, wiring, plumbing and sprinkler fixtures. He also should be required to make any repairs to the interior of the premises which may be needed because of his failure to do any of the work described above.

The landlord intent upon writing a net lease will be showing excellent form in the high jump at this point, but there's more. He also should be obliged to repair and replace the parking lot and common areas as needed. This is an obligation distinctly separate from maintenance of those things, discussed earlier. It involves such major items as resurfacing the parking lot, replacing light standards and doing work upon any of the numerous subterranean utility lines required to keep the demised premises in operation.

The conditions above are most often first noticed by the tenant, which is in possession of the property. A request for repairs or replacement, very specifically worded, should be sent to the landlord by certified or registered mail. The landlord then should have 5–10 days in which to commence the work required, and complete it in a reasonable time thereafter. If he fails to do so, then the tenant should have the right of *self-help*. That is, the tenant should have the right to step in and perform any work which the landlord has failed to do and bill the cost of it to the landlord. Further, if the landlord should fail to make a full reimbursement to the tenant within 30 days, the tenant should have the right to deduct that sum, plus allowable interest, from future rent payments. Expect explosions over self-help, but it is worth fighting for, and should include the common areas as well as the building.

The tenant should accept an obligation to make repairs to the interior of the demised premises, meaning wall, partition and ceiling surfaces, doors, floor coverings and, usually, all plate and other types of window glass. This obligation should be carried out well enough so that the tenant can, at the end of the lease term, yield up the demised premises in a condition comparable to that at the beginning of the term, reasonable wear and tear, damage by fire or the elements, or other casualties beyond the tenant's control excepted. If the tenant has won a self-help right, expect the landlord to demand one. Tie it, of course, to notice and performance periods.

It is not enough, over the course of a full lease term, merely to keep the interior in good condition. The tenant, from time to time, will desire to make alterations to the premises, in the process of what is usually referred to as remodeling. This should be stated as a right rather than an obligation, a right exercisable at any time without the landlord's review or consent unless the work involves structural modifications. Thus the tenant should be able to move partitions and non-bearing walls as well as change its fixture layout plan and decor package. But the moment proposed work cuts into a structural element of the premises, the landlord should have the right to review and approve of plans.

When an addition to the building is contemplated, a negotiating situation is created which could lead to a substantially new lease. Thus the tenant should secure the right, though not the obligation, to construct and pay for building additions itself, within the framework of landlord review and consent. It is also nice to have, though increasingly difficult to get, a reserved area next to the demised premises, intended solely to accommodate a future addition by the tenant. While the right to construct and pay for an addition can have certain occupancy cost advantages, remember that the improvements become the property of the landlord. An addition is a topic which is approached most meaningfully in the context of a specific situation.

UTILITIES

The expense of utility services consumed within the demised premises belongs exclusively to the tenant. *Within* the premises, as measured by its own separate meter. Do not confuse this with the expense of providing and maintaining those services up to the demised premises, which belongs exclusively to the landlord.

INSURANCE

The provision of insurance should be a split responsibility. Since the landlord owns the property, require him to insure it against *fire and comprehensive casualties*. Request coverage to the extent of full replacement value; do not accept less than 90% of same. If the supermarket is part of a shopping center, the landlord also should carry *public liability* insurance covering the common areas. The landlord will seek to load the premium payments for both types of insurance into the tenant's common area expenses. Yield to him only on public liability, and seek to have that cost deducted from percentage rent obligations. The tenant also should carry public liability insurance covering the demised premises and, if freestanding, the entire property. Amounts of coverage should be dictated by common sense with an eye to court awards: $1,000,000 single limit coverage seems to be popular for public liability in 1982.

What happens if events translate insurance from coverage to

claim is usually a lengthy, separate Article in the lease, and is almost exclusively the product of a learned member of the legal profession.

USE AND RESTRICTIONS

The legal profession, in fact, really takes over the lease from this point onward. Consider the topics of use and restrictions. It was once common to meander broadly in those areas when constructing a lease. But the test of operation showed that people were getting burned by agreements they'd entered into. For instance, the decision to shut down a store with heavy losses would run afoul of a lease covenant which required continuous operation as a supermarket. Or a superb location might come within reach, but be two miles from a store where the lease forbade construction of a sister unit within three miles of it. As a result, many agreements upon use and restrictions have been paraded into court and contested. Very often the courts have ruled against the effects of such agreements, citing objections such as excessively punitive penalties and attempts to limit the development of trade. The lease should be free of such covenants. If either party insists upon them, they should recognize that enforcement is doubtful and a court appearance is possible.

DAMAGE, DESTRUCTION AND RESTORATION OF PREMISES

Certain parts of a lease hopefully will never be tested by circumstances. One is the Article which treats damage, destruction and consequent restoration of the demised premises. No matter how carefully the Article is constructed, every "what if" cannot be treated, and such a casualty most often produces operational headaches and a legal mess.

Amidst the complexities, the tenant has some basic objectives:

1. To be sure that all insurance proceeds are used for restoration of the premises. If those are inadequate, the excess cost must be borne by the landlord.

2. To be sure that the restoration will be commenced and completed as quickly as possible.

3. To be sure that no rental or other occupancy expense will be paid while the premises are unfit for the tenant's use.

Winning those rights for the tenant is never easy, nor does it end the battle. The whole Article is a chess match, and when one party makes a move it should expect the other to counter smartly. This being composed for the tenant's benefit, here are a few shadings of the variations which normally arise from the basic objectives stated above:

1. If the store has been losing money, or is nearing the end of its lease term without a promising future, the tenant will want the right to terminate the lease rather than restore the premises.

2. If for any reason the landlord fails to complete restoration work, the tenant will want the right, though not the obligation, to do so; and to deduct the cost of that work from future rental payments.

3. If the premises are but partially damaged and the tenant is able to use the remainder to conduct its business, it will want rent and other charges to abate proportionately until restoration work has been completed.

The list goes on. What if everything in a shopping center burns down except the tenant's store? Whatever the request, the landlord usually retreats to a simple but effective defense: he shrugs his shoulders and says that he understands, but that his lender never permits such things in a lease. The lender usually is cited in a tone of voice reserved for conversation in a chapel. The wise tenant has, in an earlier session, told his own lawyer what positions he *must* take to win this Article. Secure in that, it is an excellent time to go out for a cup of tea and a little sandwich, leaving the attorneys to slash and hack at each other's phrases.

CONDEMNATION

If the earlier session has been lengthy and thorough enough, the tea break can extend right through the Article which treats condemnation, or the taking of property by power of *eminent domain.*

Such things *do* happen. The state widens the highway out front from two to four lanes, and there goes an important piece of the parking lot, and perhaps a vital curb cut as well. The county declares that its studies demonstrate that your supermarket sits astride the most logical place for it to build a sewage treatment facility. If a government agency can demonstrate that its purposes have a higher social benefit than retailing, a condemnation and taking may follow.

The tenant's concerns vary according to whether the whole property is taken or only part of it. If the whole property goes, the lease should terminate upon the date of taking. If only part of the property is taken, the tenant still should have the right to terminate the lease if it determines that it cannot continue to conduct its business at a suitable level of volume and profit on the diminished property. If the business can survive at a satisfactory though reduced level, the tenant should have the right to secure a reduction in its occupancy expenses through either negotiations or arbitration.

When a property is condemned, the authority involved must pay for the value of the land it takes, and what amount to damages for the buildings and improvements thereby rendered useless or only partially usable. The landlord, naturally, believes that all such payments belong to him. Not always. If the tenant has constructed improvements or additions to the building at its own expense, it must have the right to claim an award equal to the unamortized value of that work. Beyond that, the tenant must have the right to pursue its own claims against the taking authority. Prominent in the pursuit will be the amount of profits it might have earned if it had remained in undisturbed possession of the premises for the full length of the lease term. Of lesser value, but still significant, is the tenant's expense of removing and relocating its inventory, fixtures and equipment. The latter two items just may lose all practical value if removed from the place of occupancy.

DEFAULT

It is wholly justifiable for the tenant to pursue the self-help right discussed earlier, for the landlord always gets a massive kind of one in the Article which treats potential defaults by the tenant in the performance of its lease obligations.

The tenant must expect to face a default condition if it fails to make timely payment of rent or any other monetary charges specified by the lease. But honest mistakes occur, especially as the company grows larger. In such instances, the landlord must serve written notice of the delinquency, and the tenant should have at least 15 days to cure the problem by making full payment. Failing to do so, a condition of default then would exist.

The tenant also should expect to face a default condition if it is declared bankrupt or insolvent, or is placed in the custody of a trustee or receiver. Such conditions should not automatically trigger a default and consequent remedies, however. If the tenant somehow continues to meet its obligations under the lease, the lease should remain in full force and effect. At any rate, a recent supermarket bankruptcy demonstrated that the landlord is not entitled to immediate repossession of the premises, even if so provided in the lease.

The foregoing summarizes the only conditions which are serious enough to trigger a default. Beware of catch-all phrases, such as "or any other obligations which this lease requires the tenant to perform." That could lead to an unhappy landlord declaring a default because the tenant has failed to remove rubbish from the sidewalk in front of its store. He probably would not win in court, but who needs to suffer such annoyances?

A condition of default is grave because it then affords the landlord specific remedies. The tenant should seek to limit those remedies to the right to repossess the premises, terminate the lease and collect unpaid past rent. Few landlords are willing to stop there. If 10 years remain on the lease, they seek to keep the tenant liable for payment of 10 years' future rent. This is where the matter of "additional rent" can raise its ominous head. If, earlier in the lease, payments for real estate taxes, percentage rent and common area maintenance were described as additional rent, the tenant in default may now face liability for future payments of "minimum and additional rent" without remembering what actually constitutes additional rent.

Another favorite remedy of landlords is the right to accelerate rent, which means that the 10 years of future rent becomes due and payable at the time of default. Avoid that penalty at any cost. Also, expect the landlord to seek recovery of any expenses which might arise from repairing, redecorating and re-leasing the premises, along with all associated legal fees. The list goes on, given final shape and length by the predatory instincts of the landlord's lawyer. Remember that the only thing which entitles the landlord to those superfluous remedies is the tenant's weakness at the negotiating table.

SUBORDINATION AND NON-DISTURBANCE

When the language becomes ponderous, the parties are frequently trading rights. Witness these topics.

A leased supermarket, whether it stands by itself or is part of a shopping center, most probably has been financed by a long term loan. The lender, through the landlord, quite rightfully will insist that the lease be made subject and subordinate to the lien upon the property which the loan represents.

The tenant should accept that condition, but demand that its lease also be recognized as a lien upon the demised premises, subordinate only to the lien of the lender's loan. Further, that as long as the tenant fulfills its lease obligations, its lease rights shall not be terminated and its possession of the premises shall not be disturbed, by either the landlord or the lender or any successor to their interests. Most leases grant what is described as the right of quiet enjoyment to the tenant, but stop short of granting undisturbed possession. The latter right is especially important to have during inflationary times. Without it, imagine the prolonged struggle for possession which could ensue if an unfriendly party acquired title to the property and announced that the property's fair rental value was double the amount being paid.

SUBLEASING AND ASSIGNMENT

When all of the major terms and conditions of the lease have been stated, there still remains the very important topic of subleasing and assignment, the power of the tenant to transfer its leasehold interest, in part or in total, to another party.

It used to be standard that the tenant could sublease or assign freely, provided that it remained liable for the performance of all terms and conditions specified by the lease. Now the tenant usually must seek the landlord's written consent to the intended transaction, and be happy if that is the only condition imposed upon the transfer. This is another Article where the length depends upon the creativity and appetite possessed by the landlord and his attorney. Try to understand their position. Many a property owner has seen his tenant pocket the surplus rental from a sublease. Inflation changed everything.

MISCELLANEOUS

The lease winds down by treating miscellaneous provisions. The following seem to appear most frequently:

- Fixtures and equipment are and remain the property of the tenant, and may be removed from the premises at any time during the lease or at the termination of it.

- Any notices required by the lease must be in writing, and served by certified or registered mail.

- Neither party to the lease waives any rights it may have by failure to act immediately upon a given situation.

- The lease constitutes the total and only agreement between the parties, and can be changed only by a written amendment of it.

- The lease does not constitute a joint venture or a partnership between the parties to it.

- The lease is binding upon the respective parties to it, and upon any successors to their interests.

- There was no broker involved in the transaction. Or, if a broker did participate, the party responsible for payment of his fee is named.

The whole exercise would be wasted if the landlord and tenant did not seal the lease agreement by affixing their signatures and the date to it. The signatures should be properly witnessed and notarized, so that the document can be recorded.

```
o  o  o  o  o  o  o  o  o  o  o  o  o  o  o  o  o
  o  o  o  o  o  o  o  o  o  o  o  o  o  o  o  o
o  o  o  o  o  o  o ACQUIRO  o  o  o  o  o  o  o
  o  o  o  o  o  o  o  o  o  o  o  o  o  o  o  o
o  o  o  o  o  o  o  o  o  o  o  o  o  o  o  o  o
  o  o  o  o  o  o  o  o  o  o  o  o  o  o  o  o
o  o  o  o  o  o  o  o  o  o  o  o  o  o  o  o  o
```

9

The Retailer as Developer

Anyone who plows through a full commercial lease can't help concluding that there are definite advantages to owning the property. It is in such unguarded moments that retailers decide to become developers.

There *are* sound arguments in favor of owning your real estate, some financial, others strategic in nature. He who contemplates the developer's role for better reasons than avoiding the paperwork of a lease should also consider carefully the basic efforts and expenses which attend development.

ACQUIRING PROPERTY

If the field work phase of the planning study was done thorougly there will be a long list of desirable properties to investigate.

But it is one thing to desire a property and another to acquire it. People usually aren't inclined to sell just because a handsome stranger approaches bearing money and a statement of noble intentions. Negotiations can go on for months, even years. When charm and cash finally win out, call in your lawyer with a purchase option agreement.

After all that effort, why not buy the property immediately rather than wait another 90 days or six months? Because some condition may exist which would inhibit or prohibit development. Your lawyer will get busy with a title search and any petitions which may be required relative to zoning or building codes. Your construction and engineering staff will draft a site plan, with the ultimate objective of winning planning board approval. At the same time, they will hire a contractor to make test borings of the soil. Nothing is more disturbing than to find you've purchased a peat bog covered by a veneer of clay or gravel. Are you sure that gas, water, sewer and electric hookups are available? Now is the time to dot i's and cross t's. Some of those tasks can be approached while negotiating, but most require the time provided by purchase option control of the property. All should be written into the option as purchase contingencies.

It is important, further, to have the right to extend the option period. Perhaps your lawyer has discovered a serious title flaw, or a deed restriction which must be removed prior to development. The planning board may have expressed 90% admiration for your plan, but sent you out to engage the services of a traffic consultant or a professional architect before delivering the final 10% of its commitment. Tell the architect to stick around; you'll need him to prepare working plans for construction.

FINDING OTHER TENANTS

The period between purchase and construction is anything but a restful interlude. Seven acres is really too much for just a supermarket, so you're going to build a small strip center. This may be a good time to call in a professional developer, work out a lease agreement upon the supermarket and sell the whole project to him. Otherwise, the search for several capable, financible tenants begins, and in time you'll be juggling several sets of construction plans and leases. Some of the leases will be unbelievably tough: don't those guys realize that a landlord has to make a profit too? Perhaps we need to draft a second standard lease, one that expresses the landlord's point of view. If a leasing agent must be hired to help out, it's a sign that the company needs to assemble its own development subsidiary.

FINANCING THE PROJECT

Welcome to the world of finance. Not a shovelful of earth has been turned over yet, but you're looking at bills for real estate taxes, title insurance and professional fees of all kinds, not to mention the purchase price of the land itself. The accounting department is asking you what kind of return you expect from this project, and whether you intend to finance it with internal cash flow or an external loan. If you go internally, you'll marvel at the amounts of time required to prepare informational schedules and attend meetings, meetings, meetings. If you go externally, your life and all those unbelievable stories in the financial journals suddenly collide. There are no more fixed rate, long term loans available. Your lender wants to become your partner, and demands equity in the project. All that only after you agree upon a short term construction loan, at something like two or three points above prime. What a relief it will be to put the project out to bid, award contracts and commence construction. Before you do so, be sure that one of your meetings is with the insurance department, so that you're covered during as well as after construction.

SITE WORK

The total project begins to display discernible edges. Engineering studies and building plans are complete: it's time to put a precise price tag upon the endeavor. Put on your contractor's hat and gather up the bids. The scope of the work suddenly becomes mind-boggling; now you discover a cost component which must be added to the obvious items of land acquisition and building construction. It's called site improvement, and it has a thousand heads. The land may have buildings upon them: demolish them and haul them away. The land may be imperfectly contoured: cut it down or fill it up. Once a suitable construction pad emerges, an intriguing number of trenches must be cut into it to lay utility and drainage lines, all coordinated precisely with the building foundation work, which in itself involves some elements which surprise the apprentice developer. At last a familiar item appears on the bid sheet—paving. If you didn't realize it before, you do now: underneath the smooth top layer of asphalt there's a rough binder coating and several inches of gravel. Add lighting, striping, curbing, fencing and signs and the site work is complete. Well, not quite. The planning board really does expect that you'll landscape the project in accordance with the handsome plans which won its approval. No, you probably can't substitute arborvitae for the three-inch diameter pin oaks.

CONSTRUCTION

The rest is absurdly simple, or is it simply absurd? Gangs of contractors arrive, and vertical planes arise from the horizontal. Who coordinates all this activity, to be sure that when the cement contractor arrives, the trenching contractor will have completed his labors? You, the developer, do. Who rides herd on every phase of the job, to be sure that the money being paid out buys exactly what the plans and specifications and carefully worded contracts call for? You, the developer, do. If you don't have the time and/or expertise to function in this capacity, you hire a professional to supervise your interests. Another layer of expense, covered by the contingency funds which you *of course* factored into your financial planning worksheet.

Somehow it all gets done, even though the electrical contractor goes belly up in the middle of things. You contemplate the property file, and wistfully note that it's eight times as thick as a simple lease file would have been. But there's that glow of achievement: the buildings are complete and the tenants all in, first rental paid and ready to go on December 1. Grand Opening! Miss Hardscrabble County, free balloons, hot pizza wedges and volume beyond expectations! An untroubled night's sleep for a change. But the phone rings at six A.M. Four inches of snow fell after midnight. Damn! You totally forgot about hiring someone to handle snow removal and other common area work.

None of the foregoing is meant to serve as a horror story, but rather to illustrate that the developer must deal with a formidable body of complex tasks before the first display of lettuce can be constructed.

OWNING VERSUS RENTING: PROS AND CONS

Which route should be taken? There is no set answer, and indeed any company about to embark upon a long-range growth plan should try both. Those who prefer to be tenants argue that it allows them to focus all their resources—human and capital—upon their primary business of retailing. That is true: the company which chooses to develop and own soon confronts the necessity of creating its own property development subsidiary; and in that lurks the risk that the goals and activities of the subsidiary will control those of the parent. The tenant company, on the other hand, merely moves in when the building is ready, and its actual capital investment is limited to equipment and inventory. Thus, more stores can be opened with a given amount of capital. Again, true; but remember that accounting standards now require that the full rental obligation of a long-term lease, discounted to present value, be treated as a capital investment.

The company which prefers to develop and own will concede the complexity and risk of its position, but will cite many advantages, beginning with the ability to build when and where it wants to, and at costs fully visible to itself. After completion of a project, the owner collects rent, utilizes tax advantages and contemplates the residual value of the property far down the road. Special bonuses come when its own sales volume matures and the owner-operator gets to keep $50,000 which, as tenant, it would have paid out to the landlord for percentage rent. Or when, in a cash crunch, it sells the property for double what it cost to develop.

Something new and different may well emerge from the cocked hat created after 1980 by double digit inflation and interest rates. And that might be joint ventures between retail companies and small but professional developers. The latter have always thrived upon their exceptional skills and their ability to find passive institutions willing to make large, long-term loans at fixed rates. Those developers, unless they now wish to take on lenders as equity partners and thereby increase rentals or diminish their own rewards, have been left principally with their skills. It seems likely that retail companies with capital resources for development will find a way to combine those assets with developers' skills, especially their driving ability to get things done.

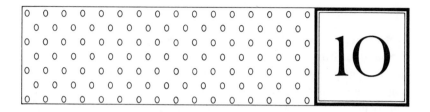

10

Assembling
the Plan

Begin by completing the assessment of your existing stores. This should commence with a study of the lease term summaries prepared earlier. What are the current annual monetary obligations related to occupancy, including rent, percentage rent, real estate taxes and common area maintenance? How many more years remain upon the current term of lease? Are there options to renew the lease? If so, for how many more years and upon what terms? What does the lease say, if anything, about the right to remodel and expand? Is there a reserved expansion area? The object of this exercise is to see whether the contract your company signed years ago will be a help or hindrance if you decide that a particular store merits improvements. There is no standard in this respect: some leases put you in the driver's seat, others drop you into the waiting jaws of a landlord.

Where properties are owned, the company obviously has a

greater degree of flexibility. Nevertheless, pull out the property files and go through all the documents. Strange covenants exist in deeds, and peculiar agreements sometimes get made when mortgages are created. Be sure that there are no encumbrances to any improvement action which may be contemplated, not the least of which could be the outstanding mortgage balance relative to a big expenditure such as a major expansion of the building.

STORE OPERATING STATEMENTS

Proceed onward to a study of operating performance for each store, beginning with the five-year record of sales and earnings, or sales and contribution, if that is your particular bottom line. Figures that go upward steadily, in excess of inflation, generally identify units which warrant further investments. But don't turn away automatically from a flat or declining performance: you may be looking at the most obvious and overdue need for physical improvements.

There is more to this phase of analysis than a study of earnings or contributions. During the Seventies, "bottom line" and other expressions of wisdom focusing upon those words became the most tiresome cliches in American business. There was a certain mystique attached to the term. It came to be that even absolute fools could—and did—utter it and command respect. The bottom line, in a real sense, is merely a remainder, what is left over as a consequence of all the lines above it, starting with sales, moving on to margins and continuing through fixed and variable expenses.

The operating statement is analagous to a thorough annual physical exam. It provides a complete look at the object under scrutiny. A line-by-line analysis will isolate any performances which depart significantly from company and industry standards. The object of the study, again, is to identify any factors which speak out for or against making an investment in a particular store. Why do we have such a high advertising cost? Perhaps we need two more stores in the ad area more than just a single expanded unit. Why has the total gross margin been so brutally thin here for the past two years? Perhaps the area is badly overstored, or perhaps we need serious in-store operational analysis before we commit to added investment. Why is our percentage rent so high? My God! You mean we pay 1½% of sales forever, with no deductions? Our real estate taxes are what? Those are the kinds of questions and possibilities which can arise from every line of the operating statement. Some are not serious enough to postpone development plans—cost of store supplies, for example—but some are. If a store has a very low sale-per-customer performance, it is tempting to say that an expanded store could double its sales by selling more to the same customers. Maybe so, but it also is possible that the store has and will have a convenience function on the retailing landscape, no matter what its size may be.

Beyond the lease and beyond the operating statement there is yet another important factor to consider. Most companies have a habit of doing numerous small remodeling jobs on one store over a period of years. Consequently, when a major job is contemplated, it often is a shock to discover the unamortized value of equipment and leasehold improvements attached to a particular unit. If you discover that there's still $250,000 on the books for a store that looks like an old tweed jacket with patches, at least absorb the lesson. If a store has real potential, do the full job all at one time and get something which resembles a new supermarket.

PRELIMINARY PLAN FOR EXISTING STORES AND NEW LOCATIONS

Prepare a list with column headings of:

- Expand
- Remodel
- No Change
- Close

Yes, Close. There will be weeping and wailing, a district manager or two may get violent temporarily. But if your company has 20 stores or more, you're probably going to confront the fact that change has its negative aspects too. Even if one of the units to be closed is at the very location where Uncle Walt trimmed his first pork chop in 1913. Enter each existing store in its appropriate column, as determined by the research done thus far. There is no need to assign precise dollar costs to each project yet, beyond, perhaps, classifying "remodels" as either major or minor. Nor is there any need to assign priority values yet. Both exercises will become critical parts of giving final shape to the development plan.

As an adjunct to this list, pull together all the information gathered about potential acquisitions, and make another list with the same column headings. If you have any illusions about making an acquisition and sailing off into some mellow sunset, forget them. Everybody's supermarkets go through the same cycles of change as your own do, and if you acquire 20 stores somewhere you'd better have the funds to do four or five major remodeling jobs upon them in the next two years.

Finally, the Christmas list of potential new locations assembled in the office and in the field should be added to the lists which express future plans for existing facilities. The initial grand product usually is something which, when rough dollar values are attached, looks like a worksheet for the national defense budget. Very often, in fact, operational people will lapse into military metaphor when called upon to defend the scope of their proposals. They will cite "The Enemy"—always 12 feet tall and endowed with inexhaustible resources—in contrast to their own wretched position, which is face down in the trenches and desperately short of bullets.

THE FIRST PROJECTION OF CAPITAL REQUIREMENTS

Learn to recognize good amateur theatrics: from here onward there must be an uncompromising devotion to mental toughness and objectivity. It is time to start pouring wishes into the mold of financial capabilities. Calculate, at present dollar values, the cost to develop during the next five years all the new stores, expansions and remodels on the grand lists. Assume for now that all new stores will be leased, thereby limiting long term cash outlays to equipment and such leasehold improvements as signs and decor. Assume for now that all expansions and remodels will be financed fully by your company—your construction department can provide an average cost per square foot of building addition. Do not include, at this point, the probable cost of any possible acquisition. It is vital to have the means to put one's own house in order before extending tentacles toward another house. Do not include, at this point, the cost of support equipment such as trucks.

Suppose that it all adds up to $100 million, or 20 million per year. Look backward and see what the company spent per annum during the past five years purely for store development projects. If the figure is $10 million, either the Christmas list is in trouble or you commence to ponder the idea of a special borrowing program, which is a full topic in itself. If the figure is $25 million, proceed to the list of potential acquisitions. If the figure is $18 million, call in the financial staff and see if they can't scratch up another $2 million per year in-house.

Whatever the calculations may add up to, go over the development proposal lists thoroughly. Compel the authors to defend each project with facts. Where facts do not exist, assume fantasy, and put the project aside. The personality of each proponent will quickly show a relation to his or her list. The supervisor from District #3 obviously knows the territory in depth and has been making mental and physical notations about development opportunities for a long time, while the person in District #7 is the type who never describes a location as bad until after the supermarket is operating upon it. In this way the lists will be pared down toward reality, and it's not bad news by any means to discover that there *are* a few stores which can go on forever with an occasional paint and decor job, and new equipment purely when needed.

PLANNING HUMAN NEEDS

Money isn't everything, even if most people act as though it is. The wishes also must be poured into the mold of human capabilities. If the exercise above produces a rough outline of 10 new stores per year, does your system, as examined earlier, have the ability to attract and develop that many store managers? If not, halt all planning activity until it does. Certainly no company possessed of its collective sense would invest $2,000,000 or more in a new supermarket, staff it with a hundred or so employees, fill it up with $500,000 worth of inventory and then hand the keys to an unknown quantity.

Human needs spread in all directions, and don't assume that just because someone is covering a certain function well in the office or warehouse that that person can handle whatever load increase comes as a result of growth during the next five years. It's tempting to say that three buyers can buy for 100 stores as easily as for 75, but that's rather shallow thinking. What if expansion takes the company into new realms of competition? The demands placed upon the buying staff could change drastically, possibly require the presence of a new person involved in new activities. What must be done is to make that sort of assessment department by department, person by person, with an eye always toward the new situations which could arise as growth progresses.

This also is the time to be sure that the company's departmental structure makes sense functionally. It is amazing how the necessities of the moment, compounded over years, cause functions to blur and overlap. Define and separate, cut, add and reassign. Do whatever it takes to give the beast sleek form. One always expects to find, during this type of exercise, areas of functional duplication and consequent reductions in overhead. Don't be myopic. It's equally important to discover gaps in functional coverage, things that aren't getting done at all.

Don't depart from this realm until the whole system of rewards is put into sensible shape. Any company which makes ambitious growth plans while preaching the same old sermons about limiting compensation growth to a miniscule percentage per annum is building castles in the sand. An ambitious growth plan puts enormous burdens upon the people who are expected to carry it out, in addition to the challenges which it represents. Reward them well for successful performances, and don't think that gross pay is all those folks care about. Be sure that the promotion ladder from within truly is open to all heights. There is little more frustrating to a talented, ambitious employee than to know that when a significant position opens up the company will go outside to fill it. Provide incentives which will give people reasons to push their performance levels into the stratosphere. Don't let stock options become the private preserve of the top few people in the company. Senior management which tosses crumbs down from the table and persists in blather about the primacy of stockholder interests might as well limit its plans to one-year periods. Who is more important to the daily and long term health of a company: the investor who owns $10,000 worth of stock or the dedicated, capable employee? If the answer is slow in coming, call up the investor and ask if he'd mind working in store operations for a month.

PLANNING SUPPORT FACILITIES

You've roughed out a plan to build, say, about 25 new stores and to remodel or expand 50 or so existing units during the next five years. You've got, or can get, the capital required for property and equipment; and you have, or can attract,the people essential to the program. Don't forget to plan for support facilities.

It can start with a decision to build or expand a warehouse, or perhaps to rent one. Or perhaps to get out of the distribution business and cast your lot with that fine wholesaler you've been talking to for the past few weeks. If you're very lucky, the warehouse or warehouses you have now will be able to service the planned development program without being expanded. No blanket recommendation can be made here. Ten different companies will reach 10 different decisions. Some cannot conceive of being in the retail business without owning and operating a warehouse; others look upon a warehouse as a constant drain upon capital and human talent.

The key to planning for support facilities is a solid estimate of the sales and tonnage increases which can be expected as a result of the development program. A precise sales projection will be made later on for each site as it is developed, but for the moment averages drawn from experience will suffice. The company, experience tells you, really needs a start-up volume of, say, $8,000,000 per annum to justify the construction of a new supermarket. What it actually has achieved over the past five years, you find, is an average of $8,500,000 in present dollars. Twenty-five new stores equals $212,500,000 in annual sales. Not all of that will be new volume: subtract instances such as where a new store will replace one currently doing $3,500,000. When all of those calculations are done, extend the same exercise to projected expansions and re-models of existing stores. Again, for now, experience is the guide. Store expansions have been providing, say, an average net sales increase of $4,000,000 per annum, while remodels have been producing an average net increase of half that figure. Add it all up to see what it looks like five years hence as a net, non-inflationary sales increase.

While that's being done, warehouse management will be getting quite nervous about translating all the sales growth into projected tonnage increases. To those people, the new store is measured not so much in sales as in the tonnage of merchandise the warehouse must be able to ship out to it week after week. Tonnage, of course, is a comprehensive term. Critical situations usually are measured within its component factors, such as the number of cases of dry groceries shipped. When warehouse management has finished defining projected sales growth in terms of tonnage, the degree of strain likely to be placed upon the warehouse will swim into view. If dry grocery operations presently is shipping a number of cases which represents 90% of the in-out capacity of the warehouse,and the development program projects a 40% increase in that number, a need for new dry grocery warehouse space exists. The same may be true for meat, produce, dairy or frozen food, if the company warehouses any of those items. But before any kind of calipers are applied to the apparently necessary new space, be absolutely certain that the old space is not concealing it. Time may have produced a very inefficient layout; old equipment may be preventing a maximum vertical use of space.

It is at this point that the marriage or renewal of vows with a wholesaler may occur, especially when the company involved has about 20 supermarkets and is starting to think seriously about owning a warehouse for the first time. The catalyst is the projected expense of acquiring, say, 12 acres of good, industrially zoned land with proper rail and highway service, and then building a 300,000 square foot warehouse-office complex thereupon. Don't forget the racks, fork lifts and office equipment; and if you've always wanted an automated warehouse to play with, an appropriate salesman will be delighted to provide quotes. The shock sometimes comes when the expense of expanding a warehouse is added up, and it becomes clear that the cost approaches the tab for a totally new facility. The basic problem with expansions, and it applies to supermarkets even more ferociously, is that you are compelled to renovate the older space substantially in order to make it compatible with the new.

At this point, the planner should know the approximate capital outlay required to construct and improve the store and warehouse facilities called for by the development program. One more major item of hardware that must be dealt with is the trucks which provide the functional link between warehouse and store in the chain reaching from producer to consumer.

Trucks are another item which divide people into sharply defined schools of thought. Some companies cannot stomach the capital expenditure which one rig represents, and so rent their fleets. Others, equally unhappy with direct involvement in union wrangling and maintenance work, trust their fortunes to contract haulers. Those who do business with a wholesaler have their feet in both those streams. And then there are those who couldn't face this competitive world unless they owned their truck fleet. Each approach can be the right one, depending upon the full situation involved; but the company which chooses to own now must translate that preference into capital requirements.

97

The proper place to begin is the realization that even if the company doesn't develop a single new store facility during the next five years it still will have to replace part of its fleet. While the transportation department is massaging that fact into a number, begin to analyze the new distribution patterns which the development program is likely to create. There will be some economies of scale, situations where a store or two can be added into a geographically compact district without creating a need for a new set of wheels—and driver—to service them. But on the other end of the spectrum, the development program may well create a whole new geographical district or districts and, consequently, a raw demand for new transportation facilities. That possibility can go beyond trucks. Sheer distance and union contracts may suddenly create the need for a depot far from the warehouse, where drivers and equipment can be exchanged and equipment can be serviced. In the warehouse itself, an expanded fleet may require significantly expanded service facilities. It's somewhat like tossing a stone into a pond; the ripples seem to expand forever. You remember the company's first computer, and how good old Charlie put store ordering onto it in his spare time; now you have a whole roomful of machines and a rapidly expanding department of people devising ways to use them. Relax. Trucks don't have the same uncontrollable mystique about them.

Which is to say that the number of new trucks required to service the number of new stores planned can be determined with a reasonable degree of accuracy. Add that figure to the one which will be necessary to keep the existing network of stores well supplied, and the final major component of capital requirements will be known. This type of analysis can produce some bonuses as well as some shocks. The whole distribution system may have become, quietly and imperceptibly over the years, a topsy-like structure badly in need of functional streamlining.

POTENTIAL SOURCES OF CAPITAL

The *need* to expend capital, in the context of the development plan, now can be measured against the company's *ability* to expend capital, which was measured earlier in the study. If the plan calls for an expenditure of $100 million during the next five years, the company must determine whether or not that sum will strain what it considers to be an acceptable debt/equity ratio, or any other yardsticks of financial health which it considers to be important. In order to do that, the potential origins of the capital must be defined accurately. Will it come from inside or outside the company? Possibly from both directions, but in what proportions?

It is rare for a company to be able to finance its growth over a five year period wholly from internally generated capital such as retained earnings. But before galloping off into the high rate lending markets of 1982, be sure that the less obvious internal sources have not been overlooked.

Now may be the time to make a strategic redeployment of some assets brought under the microscope earlier. The outright sale of surplus properties could generate millions of dollars for development capital. They need not necessarily be plants and warehouses. A supermarket property within the city, purchased decades ago, may be functionally moribund and ready for conversion into high-rise use at a sale price which will canonize the original buyer. If the property under consideration still has significant functional value, a sale-leaseback transaction may be in order. The sale-leaseback usually generates capital for long-term use at rental costs which are effectively below conventional borrowing rates. The buyer-landlord obtains tax benefits for his high bracket position and a suitable return on his investment; the seller-tenant retains long-term control of the property at lease terms strongly controlled by his earlier position of ownership. Capital generated in this manner can be of inordinate value to the company determined to manage its own development timetable. The cash can be used to finance acquisition of Year One properties, which, when securely under control, can be sold and leased back. In that way the capital, with continual guidance from a tax advisor, can be rolled over from year to year, producing both desirable locations and controlled leases.

Another internal source of help, if done well or at all, is cash management. A retail company is a cash flow pump. Most of what flows in the front door ultimately flows out the back door, but in between there are often significant opportunities to make short-term investments with cash in transit. Larger, more mature companies usually are well aware of this, and give the function departmental recognition, right next to the people who are studying our continually changing tax laws. Younger companies eventually come upon the concept as one of life's pleasant surprises. Good cash management will not provide the same large infusion of capital as sale of surplus properties, but will over a prolonged period result in improved earnings.

Another possible source of capital within the walls, by process of policy change, is store equipment. Retailers have for a long time preferred to own rather than lease store equipment, and that preference now routinely means an investment of at least $750,000 per store. Recently accelerated depreciation schedules for such property may intensify the ownership trend, but any company involved in a long-range development program might find some advantage to leasing equipment so that it can own real estate, which has better residual value.

External sources of capital are more numerous and varied, but generally expose the borrower to higher degrees of expense and risk. There is the familiar loan situation, in which the company borrows or arranges to borrow capital at terms agreed upon between parties. During recent years this has become an unattractive option. To repeat an earlier statement, borrowers have found themselves saddled with interest rates which can float a point or two above a soaring prime rate, and with lenders—large and small—which increasingly demand an equity position.

The company can raise capital by issuing and selling stock. No interest expense attaches to the sum raised, but the parties which buy the stock have very definite visions of dividends and capital gains. The first-time seller suddenly finds that its plans, decisions and performances have become accountable to strangers. Even more serious in consequence is the fact that sale of stock is sale of equity. Increasingly after 1980, the strangers sometimes are larger fish with sharper teeth, and control of the company may fall into jeopardy. Sale of stock requires an analysis of long-term objectives as well as of financial structure. It may be healthier to pay current interest rates.

The sale of debentures often is linked in popular concept with the sale of common stock, but is quite different. Debentures are corporate bonds which usually promise a specific rate of return to the buyer and nothing more. They are an attractive way to raise long-term capital because the buyers are, to a heavy degree, institutional interests willing to accept a lower rate of return than commercial lenders. Or so the formula went until about 1980. Then stratospheric interest rates made even the most passive of investors highly sensitive to maximized returns, and the bond market, corporate as well as municipal, went into a general swoon. If buyers can be found, debentures remain an attractive source of capital at rates, even after underwriting expenses, below conventional loan structures. But mainly for the largest and healthiest of corporations. Others may have to sweeten the offering with a bonus, such as a few shares of stock with every bond unit purchased.

As the conventional bond market collapsed, retail development interests swung quickly and heavily toward industrial revenue bonds as a source of capital. Those bonds, given literal application, are used to finance industrial developments which create new jobs; and hence the interest paid upon them is given tax-free status. Nevertheless, developers discovered in 1980 that many states could and would permit use of the bonds for retail projects. The advantage is significant: if a conventional long-term loan costs 15% annual interest, an industrial revenue bond issue can generate the same capital for roughly 11%. The first time venturer will see some of that spread eaten up by the learning experience and legal fees— four separate sets of attorneys may be involved—but a sizeable raw dollar advantage remains. The trouble is that by late 1981 the Internal Revenue Service and Congress were clamoring to restrict the bonds to their original purpose, and even a Coolidge-style administration might not be able to prevent that from happening. Whatever the outcome, the company with a warehouse project in its plan should be able to pursue this attractive method of financing. It should realize, however, that the transaction is somewhat of a sale-leaseback. The property developed is pledged to secure the issue, and cannot be sold or used for financial leverage in any way until the bond obligation is retired fully.

Other sources are less comprehensive in application to an overall development plan. Conventional mortgage financing still can be pursued for single projects, but rates and terms since 1980 have been discouraging. All kinds of "creative" twists and turns are possible, but what usually happens now is that the majority of the amortization period gets loaded with heavy payments in order to provide a lighter payment schedule during the rest of it. The lender, naturally, does most of his talking about the lighter end.

The capital climate of the Eighties may tempt the planner to buy lottery tickets and wait for better rates, like a surfer in quest of the perfect wave. A few lottery tickets could be fun, but don't play rate cycles. If the plan makes sense, make a full commitment to it now and put together the best package of capital sources available. A year's delay might bring better rates, but those could be offset by increased costs of land, labor and materials. Worse still, what if a point or two advantage on rates came at the expense of operational momentum? Momentum is largely rooted in human attitudes, and it can be the most fragile and perishable aspect of any plan. Compared to it, $10,000,000 in borrowed capital, which no one sees or touches in hard form, is as tangible as a bowl of fruit.

11

The Final Plan

The planning process thus far has collected information and ideas from numerous and diverse sources and shaped everything into a unified purpose. The progression from general to specific, from thought to action, is now at the final stage.

THE CAPITAL BUDGET

The first step is to prepare a capital budget with hard edges, a financial blueprint shorn of fancy, vague wishes and unfocused sentiment. The company knows that the development projects which emerged from the plan will require expenditures of $100 million during the next five years. A sobering sum of capital, to be sure, but one which the company has determined to be available from a variety of carefully analyzed sources. The company also knows, however, that equally careful analysis of its own financial structure dictates a $90 million limit on spending during the next five years. What to do?

Such dilemmas have been and will be resolved by the figurative or literal toss of a coin, but having come this far by thought process, why not expend one more brain cell? It can be a judgment call to be sure: one company will shut off at 90 while another will stretch for the extra 10. Look in the mirror again. If the VP for Finance is standing there with arms folded and stating that an extra 10 will put a critical strain upon your debt/equity ratio or any other monetary measure wired to flashing red lights, pay attention. There may be no alternative but to go back to the lists and eliminate a few projects. Before doing that, however, be sure your VP hasn't been prone to wearing sackcloth and ashes when contemplating the future. If the danger is anything but clear cut, take a shot at the full plan and the $100 million required to raise it upon the landscape. Does anyone doubt that what costs 10 today probably will cost 15 a few short years hence?

Twenty million dollars per year for each of the next five successive years, correct? Not necessarily. How much gets spent during each year depends upon the urgency of each project and the priority which is assigned to it. Also, upon a ready flow of capital from whatever sources have been targeted.

For the moment, assume a steady pace, but realize that the capital budget for the plan must be subject to at least one formal, intense review each year.

Be aware, too, that if part of the capital is scheduled to come from the sale of assets, someone had better be able to demonstrate their saleability. The cash crunch of the Eighties caused many otherwise credible executives to write articles and make speeches of an incredible nature about the mother lode represented by surplus properties. Closer scrutiny under the pressure of attempted sale may reveal that for each treasure there is some trash, property which became surplus because it became functionally or locationally obsolete.

ASSIGNMENT OF PRIORITIES

No part of the plan is more demanding than the assignment of priorities. Get out five of the largest spread sheets available and mark successive years upon each one. Then assign each development project to a particular year by entering it upon the appropriate sheet. A simple enough procedure, but upon completion of the task you discover that human nature has prevailed and 75% of the projects have ended up in Year One. The agonies of choice. Begin again.

You've decided to expand the warehouse. But when? If it gets done in Year One there may not be much capital left that year for store projects. But must it be done then; aren't you still 10 new stores away from a critical strain upon your warehouse capacity? It really belongs in Year Three, along with its projected cost of, say, $15 million.

The assignment of priorities to store projects is a more complex task, because there are more of them vying for place and each one has separate credentials and needs. Begin by separating them into categories:

- New Store
- Expansion
- Remodel
- Close

There are several factors which affect store priority assignments; they can stand alone, interrelate or conflict.

Lease status is always of primary importance. Suppose that a location has been indicated for a new store which will replace two old stores that cannot be improved. The length of time remaining on those old store leases—assuming that they are leased—will help to determine when the new store should be built. The same can be said of an expansion or remodel project. In such a case if there is less than 10 years lease time left, including renewal options, the lease should be renegotiated to provide more time. A quick renego-tiation may not be possible. The landlord may have demonstrated that nothing happens to his property until he's been paid or promised a royal ransom.

The *physical condition* of existing stores and equipment will press in on the decisions too. Perhaps you'd like to schedule the total remodeling of a particular unit midway through the plan period. But your maintenance department tells you that the compressors are shot, the refrigerated cases break down several times each week and the roof is acting as a water filter. You move the store up a slot, where it stays until it gets bumped downward again by a store which combines physical needs with other urgent conditions.

One of which can be *competitive pressure.* You've had a fine store at a particular location for years. Now it is showing those years and two of its competitors have made improvements which have caused a decrease in sales volume. Can you afford to wait three years before sending help? Probably not, but you might have to if other situations are burning more fiercely. In this respect, nothing captures attention more strongly or more immediately than the construction of a new facility by a competitor. And nothing will wreak greater havoc upon the priority schedule over the years than such an event. Before you adjust the schedule, however, be sure that the event is real.

The *degree of opportunity* which seems to exist is another consid-eration to ponder. Certain new locations have been selected for development because the opportunities are large and immediate. Too immediate for delays. Competitors are crowding around also; the door is open, and it's important to be the first one through. The same situation can affect the timing for an expansion or remodeling project. Another major component of opportunity is potential profitability. Every company earns more per sale dollar in some areas than in others. Why give high priority to projects in areas where decent margins are hard to come by? Since every project on the lists exhibits differing degrees of opportunity, assign a value to each one. One to Five, or any preferable scale. The first time around most of them will be designated as "Ones," but then some hard values will appear.

If all those factors have been handled well, they can be scrambled by *geographical strategy*. The company simply cannot think in terms of one store project at a time, unless it happens to operate in a territory totally constituted by small, one-store cities and towns well separated from one another. Most of us must cope with large cities and metropolitan areas, where trade areas adjoin and overlap each other, and media coverage often binds them together. Thus multiple store strategy becomes significant. The company desperately needs to improve its position in the growing metropolitan quadrant northwest of a particular downtown. It has a five-star new location lined up for development in Year One. Doesn't it make sense to do, in that same year, a major expansion of store #28, which shows real promise of doubled sales? And a remodel of store #26, which otherwise might be done in Year Four? It can make sense for numerous reasons, not the least of which is the message you'll convey to customers, employees and competitors. Purpose. Commitment. Dedication. Momentum.

Geographical strategy has other dimensions, too. Part of the plan may involve *development of new territory*. The general rule is to secure the home base before galloping off into the excitement of an invasion, but there can be exceptions to the rule. That new territory may be urgently ripe. The market leader may be vulnerable due to neglect, mismanagement, complacence, change of ownership or who knows what other misfortune. The territory itself may be in the early stages of an economic boom, or, conversely, so quiescent that nobody's paying much attention to an unexciting but still viable area. Inviting conditions such as those may demand quick response. Otherwise, in this crowded, eager world, prepare to suffer the pain of standing by while someone else rushes past and slaps his money down upon the table.

Then there are *potential acquisitions:* nothing is more difficult to fit into the timetable of a long-range development plan. The moment of sale, in most instances, belongs to the seller. For that reason the workability of a plan is best preserved by keeping potential acquisitions off to one side in a special reserved status. That also applies to financial planning. For example, if 20% of the main capital budget is labeled for an acquisition, five years may pass without it happening. Or it may happen at a point in the plan when you are least prepared to divert capital and attention away from other projects. Assess potential acquisitions separately; calculate the approximate probable cost of each; prepare a distinct strategy to form acquisition capital; stay abreast of ever-changing federal regulations relative to mergers and acquisitions. The government climate in 1982 is increasingly pro-bigness, like it or not, but it would be dangerous to assume a wink-and-nod approval. The time one can spend jumping through federal hoops is in itself sufficient reason to place potential acquisitions adjacent to but outside the main framework of development planning.

The best way to make a final determination of priorities is to create a structure of values related to the weight of the factors involved, and to assign a comprehensive value to each project. It is possible to do that manually, even though the larger the company involved the more information which must be juggled, both visually and mentally. However cumbersome it may get, it is the approach recommended here because the decisions involved are so crucial to the company's long-term health. Many planners probably will prefer to program all the information into a computer and let the machine sort out values and print a schedule of priorities. A usable product can be obtained that way, but the recommendation here is to program carefully predetermined individual project values into the computer. In other words, the computer's task should be to compare and rank values, not to create them. The greatest risks in relying upon a computer at this final stage of the plan are interruption of personal attention, and the dangerous tendency to feel relieved of responsibility and further contemplation once the machine spits out its answers.

Further contemplation, in fact, should be built into the priority structure. Make a notation in the Year Four schedule to begin the entire planning process again. You didn't really expect to ascend into the clouds, all tasks completed, at the end of Year Five did you?

FLEXIBILITY AND REVIEW

In a major sense, the task of translating the plan into reality has just begun, because the world outside is not going to hang in a suspended state for five years while each element of the plan gets developed in perfect chronological succession. Unpredictable delays, frustrations and impediments will arise on the landscape squarely between aspirations and achievements. For that reason, the good plan must take on an important characteristic: it must be flexible and subject to periodic review.

The reviews should be done on a formal basis at least twice during each year, and should be conducted in the context of the plan itself, the capital budget and whatever changes might be affecting the nature of the business, such as major strategic moves by competitors or the internal desire to modify prototype store plans. The review should measure how much of the plan has been accomplished up to that point, and ask what is to be accomplished during the time period to the next review. If it all hasn't been working out to a satisfactory degree in the past, don't assume that it will in the future. Determine what is wrong and design remedial action.

Flexibility is a potentially dangerous element in the plan, and demands definition.

It does not mean the unrestricted right to rip and tear, revise and discard. It means the right—the need—to make judicious changes *within* the framework of the plan in order to preserve its integrity as a total concept.

Suppose that an expansion of store #45 is scheduled during the forthcoming six-month period. The staff reports that final lease negotiations with the landlord are at an impasse, and will not be resolved in time to put the project into its time slot. After a thorough review of plan data, the expansion of store #30, where no visible delay factors exist, is moved up into store #45's priority, with #45 dropping back to the position formerly occupied by #30. That is flexibility. It is also strong medicine for the difficult landlord, who suddenly realizes that a major capital investment upon his property has been directed elsewhere.

The elements of review and flexibility may cause some to scoff at the whole process of planning, to continue grasping at opportunities and confronting challenges when and where they arise. Those who prefer that approach should contemplate the alternative one more time. If, after five years of dedicated effort, a company has managed to effect, say, 65% of its development plan, isn't that company light years ahead of the one which has taken the slash and stab route in the high-cost, high-risk world of retailing?

THE STATEMENT OF GOALS

One step remains: to quantify the goals of all this effort.

Net sales increases were calculated earlier for each project. These figures will be used as the basis for a statement of goals, but remember that a detailed analysis and projection of sales potential should be made just before each project is launched. Sales projection is a separate, lengthy and specialized topic, and will be treated very briefly here.

Most large companies handle this function internally; smaller retailers often hire the services of consultants who specialize in this task. There are numerous effective methods for projecting sales: some are simple, some are complex; some are done manually, more and more employ computers. Select any method which you believe produces accurate results; use your own department or employ consultants. But adhere to a few guidelines. Understand the method which is being used, and *demand* that field study be part of the method. Most importantly of all, read the study and projection, and challenge conclusions if necessary. As site analysis and sales projection have grown into a specialized and increasingly computerized profession, an arcane mist has settled between the specialist and the executive. The latter too often looks to the presence of the report rather than to its contents for assurance. Avoid such mental sloppiness. Dig into the report and derive assurance from facts. Finally, be sure later on to compare performance against projection. If the results are not consistently satisfactory, seek a better sales projection method and, if necessary, better people to employ the method.

Return now to the sales projections made by employing analogies of operating experience. Simply add up net sales increases for all the projects which became part of the final plan. The sum so derived represents the goal for net sales increase generated by the plan. It then can be used to calculate the goals for increased earnings, returns on sales, investments and net assets and, finally, share of market positions.

Share of market is expressed by calculating the percentage of available supermarket dollars which your company captures in a specifically defined area. If the sales potential in Franklin County is $1,000,000 per week, and your company's two supermarkets there gross $200,000 per week, your share of market is 20%. The area defined also could be a town or a city, a portion of or an entire metropolitan area, a state or a region which includes several states.

How does one determine sales potential, which normally is expressed first in per capita terms? Actual expenditures vary broadly because of income differences, so averages are used for geographic areas as expressed above. There are numerous sources of data on supermarket expenditures. The U.S. Department of Labor prepares and updates such information on a regular basis. Firms which specialize in the sale of demographic data can provide it for areas as small as a city block. Your own company, if possessed of a research function, should make periodic samplings of expenditures by income level. In 1982 the range approximates $17.00–$23.00 per capita per week. If Franklin County has 50,000 people and an average weekly per capita expenditure of $20.00, the weekly sales potential is $1,000,000.

Through the use of such data, it is possible to state that the company's present share of market in metropolitan Charlotte, N.C. is 12%; that the goal of the development plan in that area is to raise the share to 18%. The statement can be made also about all of North Carolina or all of the southeastern United States, if the company operates or plans to operate in those larger areas. The figures, remember, are derived from current dollars and population values, and are intended to provide measures of change against current performance. In order to make share of market projections in future dollar values, one would have to be able to project accurately population, expenditure and sales increases, real and inflationary, over a five year period. That can be done, but it is a massive project and should not be permitted to clutter the planning process.

The importance of knowing one's share of market position goes beyond the dream of being "Number One" in an area. If the company is operating in a metropolitan area of less than 1,000,000 people and has a share of market position of under 10%, it's very probable that the position is a weak one, and very costly to maintain on a per-store expense basis. The same can be said of having less then a 5% share of market in a metropolitan area of more than 1,000,000 people. Thus share of market is an important measure of where you are and where you're going. If, while the plan is being assembled, you calculate that the effort will increase the share of market in Richmond, Va. from 6% to only 8%, you're not going anywhere worthwhile there. Two choices loom: either get out of Richmond and redeploy your assets elsewhere, or double your effort in that growing area and get your share of market up over 10%.

The plan is complete. Bind it with leather or paper clips according to your preference, but be sure that it becomes and remains a working document rather than a display item. Used properly, it will set people, capital, equipment and materials into purposeful motion, transforming what has been and is into what will be.

0 0 0 0 0 0 0 0 0 0 0 0 0 0 0 0 0
0 0 0 0 0 0 0 0 0 0 0 0 0 0 0 0
0 0 0 0 0 0 0 0 0 0 0 0 0 0 0 0 0
0 0 0 0 0 0 0 0 0 0 0 0 0 0 0 0
0 0 0 0 0 0 0 0 0 0 0 P&C 0 0 0 0
0 0 0 0 0 0 0 0 0 0 0 0 0 0 0 0
0 0 0 0 0 0 0 0 0 0 0 0 0 0 0 0

12

Case Study: A Profile of Planned Development

It is one thing to discuss what can and should be done to plan healthy business growth; it is quite another to step out into the confusion of the world and do those things. Here, then, is a brief outline of what one company managed to accomplish during a ten year period by carefully and continually planning its development. It is presented with the permission of the firms involved, Pneumo Corporation and its subsidiary, P&C Food Markets, Inc.

Prior to 1970, Pneumo was an industrial conglomerate with

principal operations in aerospace and machine tool manufacturing. As such, it experienced peak-and-valley earnings because of heavy startup costs and long maturity periods common to its major contracts. The decision was made to diversify into retailing in the hope that a cash flow business would help to provide a more level earnings experience year after year.

By January 1972 Pneumo had acquired three food companies which, in their contiguous territories, provided a base of operations in upstate New York, Vermont, western New Hampshire and the northern edge of Massachusetts. The first and largest acquisition was P&C Food Markets, based in Syracuse, New York, with 58 company operated and 50 franchised supermarkets, plus wholesale and institutional service divisions. Next came Saveway Markets, a 19-store chain, with operations west and north of metropolitan Albany, New York. The final acquisition was the Cross Company of White River Junction, Vermont, which added 25 company operated supermarkets, a wholesale division and a full service warehouse which was a territorial bookend to its larger counterpart in Syracuse.

This patchwork quilt of operations had an initial annual volume per store of $1,450,000; as the first year progressed it became evident quickly that painful major surgery lay just ahead. By the end of 1972 the number of company operated supermarkets had been reduced from 102 to 94 and there still existed a multiplicity of store names and merchandising policies. Total sales from food operations were $224,000,000 and annual sales per store were up to $1,750,000, but the number at the bottom of the statement wore brackets.

At this point Pneumo senior management surveyed its domain and asked, in essence, the question which commences serious planning:

What are we?

The answer was, briefly, a loosely cemented collection of generally small, old and under-equipped supermarkets. The territory—some 50,000 square miles of it—was not all that exciting either. It was, and is, a region where small cities pop up on the landscape every 20 miles or so, and the four metropolitan areas seem almost out of place. Population growth was limited to a few widely scattered suburban areas, but on the other hand there were no areas of serious and sustained population decline. The economic base presented a similar picture: only a few bright spots, but general stability. The position relative to competition was unfavorable: in almost every situation Pneumo's supermarkets ranked behind regional and local chains in terms of size, volume, merchandising punch and general customer appeal.

Armed with self-knowledge and the ability to generate development capital internally, Pneumo management proceeded to the next basic question:

What do we want to become?

The obvious answers of bigger and better had to be defined in the contexts of both the stores and the operating territory.

The stores, where locations justified it, would be remodeled, expanded and re-equipped, the precise scope of work to be governed by each situation. Those stores with significant sales potential but no physical space to accommodate it would be replaced by new units in nearby locations. Those stores with neither the potential nor the space to become high-powered chain operations would be either converted to franchised supermarket operations or discarded. The company operated stores would have a uniform name—P&C—and would be sufficiently large and well-equipped to go head-to-head against the best of their competitors. The emphasis would be on food retailing, and there would be a singular merchandising concept which customers from one end of the territory to the other could depend upon and relate to on a long-term basis.

There would be no significant expansion of the operating territory unless the opportunity to acquire all or part of another company should arise. That decision, made at a time when other companies were leapfrogging whole states with their new units, was a particularly critical one. It recognized the enormous amount of work which had to be done to make and keep P&C a major force within its own territory. In that territory, development activities would be concentrated in the non-metropolitan cities. The exception to that would be Syracuse, where P&C had both its headquarters and a large number of supermarkets as a base to build upon.

Finally, it was time to ask:

How do we get there?

As always, with people, money and ideas. The difference would be that those component forces would be applied within the framework of a consciously developed plan. Pneumo decided that the first major goal at P&C was to build up sales and merchandising skills to first-class standards. Accordingly, the melange of promotional tactics used from time to time and place to place were scrapped. The customer who formerly had to contend with trading stamps and promotional discounting in the same store awakened to a refreshingly singular concept: wall-to-wall and week-to-week low prices in every P&C supermarket.

As that program gathered momentum, other important things were done. P&C owned a large number of supermarket properties. Nearly all of those were sold and leased back, thereby generating capital for development purposes. The physical and conceptual melding of three companies into one continued onward to completion. New people were brought into P&C from a broad variety of backgrounds, thus bringing fresh perspectives to what had been a highly inbred organization. A systematic study of the entire territory was made to identify the cities and the stores where long-term potential existed, and to determine the priorities which attached to each situation. A new store logo was designed; the need for a standardized approach to store layout and decor was translated into the real dimensions of store expansions and remodelings; the variety of leases which existed were refined into a single standard form.

When the first five years of its involvement in food retailing ended, Pneumo was able to contemplate some solid achievements. Total food division sales were $378,700,000, an increase of nearly 80% over the consolidation year 1971. More importantly, the division's contribution to Pneumo's earnings was $6,900,000, which was both a healthy 1.8% of sales and proof that Pneumo's diversification plan was working. It is significant to note that while the number of P&C stores had dropped from 102 to 93, the average annual sales per store had more than doubled, reaching $3,250,000 per unit. Although the total number of P&C stores in operation had decreased, nearly $20,000,000 had been expended upon new stores, expansions and remodelings in a process of selected development. Most of that capital had been applied to company operated stores, but the franchise and wholesale sectors of the food division nevertheless had become gratifyingly profitable.

The major accomplishment of the first five years was that three separate companies which were headed nowhere individually had been welded together into a forceful entity with a future. The sales development program of wall-to-wall and week-to-week low prices was solidly established and accelerating smoothly; the task of separating the wheat from the chaff among stores and locations was progressing into productive stages. As the second five years began, it was time to add emphasis to other aspects of growth.

One of those was the systematic training and development of store personnel, a need which became critical when annual volume in several P&C stores reached $5,000,000. Thus, a long-term commitment to a personnel training and development program was made. The program, part of P&C's organizational structure, has added a professional polish to store operations and assures a continuing supply of well trained and motivated store employees.

Increased volume offers increased profit, but only if every function which becomes a line on the store operating statement receives sustained professional attention. Accordingly, P&C instituted programs in labor scheduling, energy management and warehouse inventory control, mindful of what fractions of one percent added together here and there mean in this high volume cash business. In the arena of store development, each project had to meet or surpass standards for projected returns on sales, investment and net assets.

Capital expenditures could not be lavished upon the stores alone, for increased volume and the passage of years were putting a severe strain upon support facilities. Scores of diesel tractors and

117

trailers were purchased; everything from fork lifts to computers clamored for attention. But nothing was more outgrown than the warehouses themselves. A 100,000 square foot addition to the Vermont facility was followed quickly by the leasing and subsequent purchase of a 104,000 square foot warehouse in Syracuse, which became P&C's New York meat distribution center and secondary dry grocery facility. Then, in 1981, work started on a 157,000 square foot automated warehouse addition to the main depot in Syracuse, along with expansion and renovation of headquarters office space. Those projects devoured capital, of course, and were financed in part with revenue from two bond issues.

Store development proceeded along the traditional routes of lease financing for new stores and the use of internally generated capital for remodelings. When the world of conventional financing fell apart in 1980, P&C turned to industrial revenue bonds and completed some important projects which otherwise would have remained upon the drawing board.

The end of 1981 marked the close of ten busy, productive years. Of the 91 P&C supermarkets in operation at that time, 64 were new or substantially different than they had been in 1971. Thirteen were new from the ground up; of that number, seven were replacements for older P&C's and six were in new trade areas within the territory. Thirteen additional units were new by virtue of having been acquired from other companies and remodeled extensively; five as replacements for older P&C's and eight in new trade areas. Eleven others were expanded and re-equipped, and 27 more were totally remodeled and re-equipped within existing walls. Virtually all of the remaining 27 were treated to some degree of remodeling and spot replacement of equipment. Along the way, 29 of the original group of supermarkets were closed.

Pneumo's food division sales in 1981 totaled $704,000,000, an increase of 232% during the decade of ownership. When P&C's sales of $546,000,000 are examined separately, the performance is even more impressive. Although there were fewer P&C's in operation than originally, the annual sales average had reached $6,000,000 per store, a ten year gain of 314%. Price inflation of 150% for the decade must be subtracted to obtain a meaningful measure: the real growth of 164% emerges as a highly respectable figure, especially in a territory of small cities with almost no net population or economic growth.

The sales history sketched here may be unexciting to the company which has been building superstores in the Sunbelt, or warehouse stores anywhere, but no regional differences can dim the lustre of the statistic which provides a common measure of everyone. In 1981 Pneumo's food division contributed earnings of $11,538,000, or 1.64% of sales. The growth of income during the decade cannot be stated in percentage terms, because earnings were zero when the acquired companies were first consolidated.

The Pneumo-P&C example offers something beyond the numbers involved. It teaches the importance of tailoring operations and growth to the realities of a territory. It demonstrates how planned development can breathe life into what is close to a moribund business, and create a unified force out of aimlessly diverse entities. Finally, it illustrates that opportunity can lie under one's feet as well as beyond some seductive horizon.

Index

A

Alterations and additions (landlord and tenant), 72-74
Assembling the plan, 89-102
    capital requirements, 92-93
    human needs, 94-95
    preliminary, for existing stores and new locations, 91-92
    sources of capital, 98-102
    store operating requirements, 90-91
    support facilities, 95-98
Assignment, lease, 80-81

B

"Base year" taxes, 69-70

C

Capital, potential sources of, 98-102
Capital budget, 103-104
Capital requirements, 92-93
Case study, 113-119
Commencement, of the lease, 64-65
Common area maintenance, 70-72
Company facilities, 43
Company's (existing) identity, 25-27
Competition, 7
    field study, 42-43
Condemnation, building, 77-78
Construction, 86-87
Construction improvements, 61-64
Cross section structural detail plan, 54

121

About the Author

Bernard Kane has spent half his fifty years advising business people on retail development planning, so he finally decided to write a book about it. And, no surprise, he's called the book *Retail Development Planning*.

Mr. Kane began with the best in the field, as an associate at Saul B. Cohen Associates, then moved into his own consultation work, where his clients ran the gamut from the mass merchandiser to the single-unit entrepreneur, both in food and general merchandise.

Having spent his earlier business years helping corporate structures from the outside, he moved into the executive suite in the late '60's as a real estate specialist. For the past decade he's provided expert direction to a varied collection of companies under the Pneumo umbrella, a big board conglomerate with both retailing and industrial holdings.

This is Mr. Kane's second book. The first, also for Fairchild Books, was a real mouthful—*A Systematic Guide to Supermarket Location Analysis*—but despite the name it had several successful printings and was also avidly read in the Japanese translation.

His masters degree from Boston University doesn't do him a bit of good in understanding what his oldest son has learned in high school calculus. He lives with his wife and three sons in Sudbury, Massachusetts, where he gets away—only rarely—from developers and the like, either puttering around the garden or tossing a rod and reel.